Oxford International Resources

5

Sustainability

Project Book

Jody Ellenby

Curriculum developer: Jaimie P. Cloud

OXFORD

OXFORD
UNIVERSITY PRESS

Great Clarendon Street, Oxford, OX2 6DP, United Kingdom

Oxford University Press is a department of the University of Oxford. It furthers the University's objective of excellence in research, scholarship, and education by publishing worldwide. Oxford is a registered trade mark of Oxford University Press in the UK and in certain other countries

First published in 2025

British Library Cataloguing in Publication Data
Data available

978-1-38-204758-6

10 9 8 7 6 5 4 3 2

The manufacturing process conforms to the environmental regulations of the country of origin.

Printed in Great Britain by Bell and Bain Ltd, Glasgow

Acknowledgements

The publisher and author would like to thank the following for permission to use photographs and other copyright material:

Artwork: Cover artwork by Gerhard van Wyk. All other artwork by Q2A Media. **Photos: p7:** Alessandro D'Esposito/Shutterstock; **p8 (t, l):** Triff/Shutterstock; **p8 (t, r):** Cinefootage Visuals/Shutterstock; **p9:** Ehrman Photographic/Shutterstock; **p10:** BlueRingMedia/Shutterstock; **p11 (t):** Dima Zel/Shutterstock; **p12:** Blue Planet Studio/Shutterstock; **p13:** Juergen Faelchle/Shutterstock; **p16:** Vlad61/Shutterstock; **p17:** GUDKOV ANDREY/Shutterstock; **p18 (l):** Olhunia/Shutterstock; **p18 (r):** Vastram/Shutterstock; **p19:** mhmatsu/Shutterstock; **p26:** atk work/Shutterstock; **p27 (t):** RobynCharnley/Shutterstock; **p27 (m):** Federico Rostagno/Shutterstock; **p27 (b):** Vadym Zaitsev/123RF.com; **p30:** Jester-Flim/Shutterstock; **p34 (t):** Stephen Green-Price/Shutterstock; **p34 (b):** soft_light/Shutterstock; **p35:** Davdeka/Shutterstock; **p36 (m):** George Burba/Shutterstock; **p36 (b):** Molly NZ/Shutterstock; **p37:** Robert Szymanski/Shutterstock; **p38 (t):** Marzolino/Shutterstock; **p38 (b):** zmkstudio/Shutterstock; **p39:** ChristineMinato/Shutterstock; **p40 (t):** Andrii Yalanskyi/Shutterstock; **p51 (l):** ssuaphotos/Shutterstock; **p51 (r):** Iakov Kalinin/Shutterstock; **p52 (t):** blue-sea.cz/Shutterstock; **p52 (b):** vichie81/Shutterstock; **p56 (b):** Yuriy Kulik/Shutterstock; **p60 (t, l):** Kiorio/Shutterstock; **p60 (t, r):** Stocksnapper/Shutterstock; **p60 (b, l):** Piotr Gatlik /Shutterstock; **p60 (b, r):** khuntong/Shutterstock; **p61 (t):** Juice Verve/Shutterstock; **p61 (b):** CRS PHOTO/Shutterstock; **p62 (t):** New Africa/Shutterstock; **p62 (b):** worradirek/Shutterstock; **p63:** AnnGaysorn/Shutterstock; **p64:** AB Forces News Collection/Alamy Stock Photo; **p65:** alexkich/Shutterstock; **p67:** Srdjan Randjelovic/Shutterstock; **p68 (t):** KRIACHKO OLEKSII/Shutterstock; **p68 (b):** Tomatito/Shutterstock; **p69 (t):** Santi Peloche/Shutterstock; **p69 (m):** James Michael Dorsey/Shutterstock; **p69 (b):** Reimar/Shutterstock; **p70 (t):** Frame Stock Footage/Shutterstock; **p70 (b):** Ground Picture/Shutterstock; **p72:** Lin kent/Shutterstock; **p73:** Siriussobright/Shutterstock; **p75:** Pressmaster/Shutterstock; **p76 (t):** Australian Associated Press/Alamy Stock Photo; **p76 (m):** Speed Media/Alamy Stock Photo; **p76 (b):** PA Images/Alamy Stock Photo; **p77:** Tint Media/Shutterstock; **p78 (t):** 2630ben/Shutterstock; **p78 (b):** GreenOak/Shutterstock; **p82:** SeventyFour/Shutterstock.

Contents

Project framework: IDEAS to Action

The IDEAS to Action Framework is a bit like a map to help you plan your project. There are six steps in the framework. We will cover each of these steps through the Project Book.

1. Investigate: Introduce and learn about a problem

Your goal in this section is to learn the causes and effects of the problem you are trying to solve.

2. Define: Develop solutions

Your goal in this section is to decide how you will approach the problem: what solution do you propose?

3. Explore: Experiment and test solutions

Your goal in this section is to create and test your solution and explore improvements.

4. Act: Apply, engage, and implement your solution

Your goal in this section is to make the project a reality.

5. Share: Reflect, communicate, and consider learnings

Your goal in this section is to take some time to share what you have done and reflect on what you have learned.

6. Go further! Take action for global change

Your goal in this section is to take action in your own community, or in other areas of your life, using the skills you have learned.

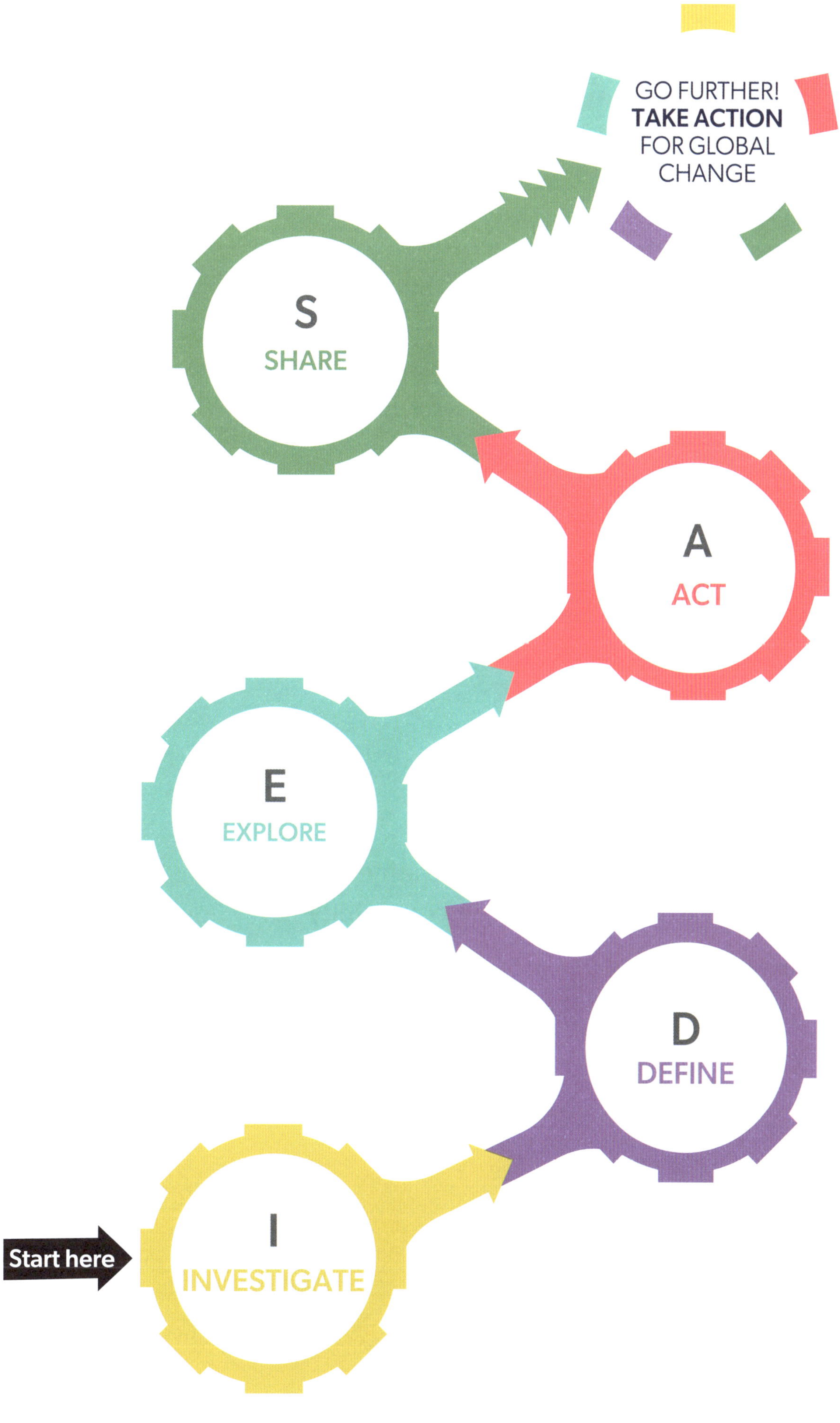
GO FURTHER!
TAKE ACTION
FOR GLOBAL
CHANGE
S
SHARE
A
ACT
E
EXPLORE
D
DEFINE
I
INVESTIGATE
Start here

1 Living on planet Earth

Contents

Dear Student,

Welcome to your first project of Year 5! Here, we challenge you to plan for the future in which you want to live.

In this project, you will explore how planet Earth works and learn about nature's basic rules. If someone buys a machine, there will be instructions to describe how it works, and if they don't follow the instructions, they may break the machine. We also need to know how Earth works so that we don't break it. You will look at the importance of understanding these laws from nature and explore ways to create a sustainable future of your own community.

Have fun exploring and working on your project!

Best wishes,

The Sustainability Team

Nature's basic rules

Look at the pictures of space and planet Earth. Share what you notice.

What are the basic conditions for life on Earth?

All life on Earth follows certain laws and principles.

Think about it! If you drop an object, it always falls. If you drop a feather, it may fall differently from how a rock falls, but all matter is affected by gravity, and this is a law in physics and science.

Why do we need to understand the laws of nature? When we know the rules that everybody in society accepts, we can predict some things. For example, we know that when traffic lights show red, everybody will stop until the traffic lights turn green. In the same way, if we know the laws of nature, we can predict some of the results of some of our actions.

Don't forget to look at the Word bank or a dictionary to find the meaning of the words you don't know.

Citizens of Earth

A citizen is a person who was born or lives in a certain place. We are all citizens of Earth!

Listen to your teacher reading out each principle. Think of some examples of this principle in action. Stand up to share an example of the principle.

Nature's laws and principles are the way that everything works and why things happen the way they do.

This list shows some of these basic rules:

- Nature uses sunlight and sugar.
- Nature works in cycles.
- Nature thrives (grows, improves, or gets stronger) on diversity.

Talk with a partner: How do the natural laws and principles affect us?

As a citizen of Earth, do you think you have rights? If you have rights, do you also have responsibilities to the planet?

Nature thrives on diversity!

Read the Welcome letter on page 7. Share your favourite part.

Create your Project Notebook. Add the project title to your notebook. Add 'My Personal Word Bank' to keep track of key words. Write down today's key words and at least one of the laws and principles from nature.

Systems within systems

Read about systems below. Then discuss, as a class, some examples of systems.

Systems have two or more parts that are connected and work together.

For example, a bicycle is a system with many parts working together. Bicycles are examples of machine systems. Engines, elevators, and cars are all machine systems.

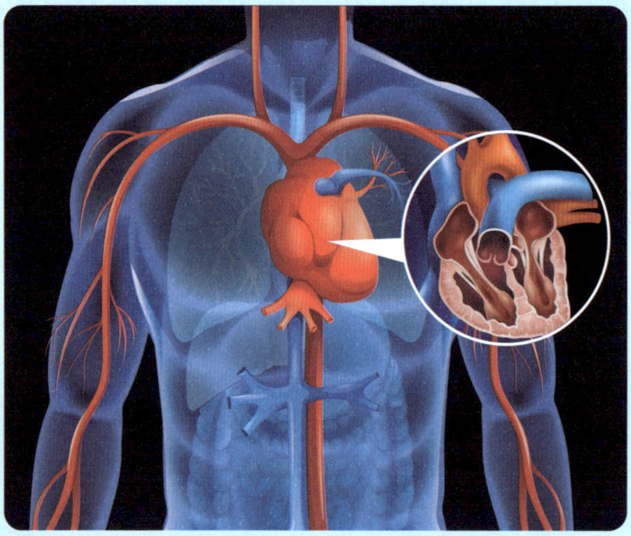

The human circulatory system

The human body is one system and has many parts, which are also systems. For example, the heart is a system with many parts (different valves and ventricles). Each part of the heart works together to bring blood in and take it out. This heart system is part of the larger circulatory system. The role of the heart in the circulatory system is to keep blood moving through your whole body and its many systems. The circulatory system is part of the larger whole-body system. Our bodies are examples of living systems.

There are some simple living systems, and some very complex living systems – systems within systems within systems.

The system could be one human organ, or one whole person, or an entire ecosystem, or our whole planet Earth!

We can better understand any living thing when we:

- identify the parts of the system
- explain how the parts of the system are connected to each other
- explain how the parts work together
- explore how the system is part of a larger system or connects to it.

Spaceship Earth

Read the following mission brief.

MISSION

Scenario: A spaceship and its crew are lost in another galaxy, which is too far for radio communication! Your task is to design and make a rescue spaceship.

Crew: As crew (people who live, work on, and control the ship), you are all responsible for the success of this mission.

Mission: You are responsible for the design of each sub-system and the larger, interconnected system of the spaceship.

Sub-systems designers: Divide your crew into pairs or small groups. Each group will design at least one sub-system. During the design process, they will need to keep checking with the other groups that all of the sub-systems function together as a whole.

Water systems: use and recycling of water

Animal quarters: live animals, fish, worms, and so on

Crew quarters: sleeping spaces, living and social spaces, happiness and needs of crew members

Solid waste systems: human and animal waste, other recycling, and rubbish containers

Greenhouse: plants for oxygen, food, medicine, and other purposes

Answer the design questions in the rescue mission activity on page 84–86.

Limits inspire creativity

Read these laws and principles from nature:

- Nature uses sunlight and sugar.
- Nature recycles everything because there is no such place as 'away'.
- Nature thrives on diversity.
- Nature uses the power of limits.
- In nature, everything and everyone is interdependent and interconnected.

Review your answers in the Rescue mission activity page. Which laws and principles from nature are important for your design? For example: Nature recycles everything because there is no such place as 'away'. How does this principle affect your design?

Complete your activity and your design, then discuss and share ideas. How did the principles influence your design and inspire your creativity?

Let's get talking

- If something 'flows', it moves in a smooth and free manner. Did you experience a flow of ideas in your group?
- Did working as a group allow the flow of ideas? If so, what added to the flow? If not, what prevented the flow?
- How could you improve the design on your spaceship to improve the flow as a whole?

Open and closed systems

All of the sub-systems of your spaceship are interconnected. In a situation like that, it is possible that the solution to one problem creates a problem somewhere else. How did you make sure that it didn't happen?

Think about when you designed your spaceship. How does your spaceship and its sub-systems compare to our whole Earth?

Look at the picture and read the descriptions below:

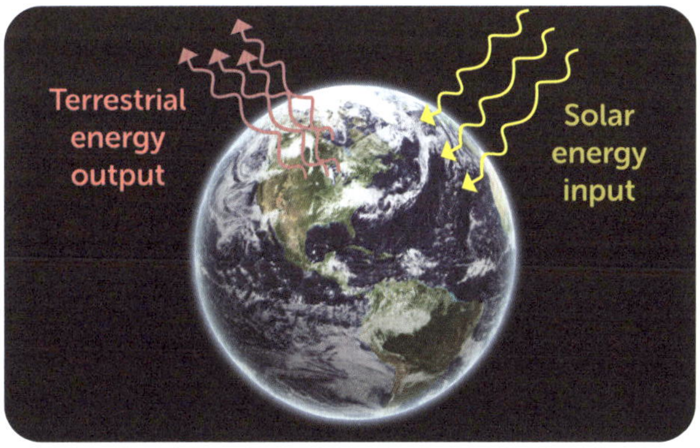

Earth as an open system

Open system for energy: Energy is radiated into Earth's system, mainly from the sun. Energy radiates back into space from Earth. Earth's atmosphere and ozone layer control the flow and balance of energy.

Closed system for materials: Earth does not get more matter or lose matter; matter just keeps cycling around and around, and it adds to life in the process. Matter does not enter or leave Earth (except for a meteorite sometimes coming in and spaceship going out). This is because of gravity. We call this the Law of Conservation of Matter.

Think about it! When you worked on your spaceship design, what type of system were you designing?

Share examples of how materials cycled on your spaceship.

Earth is a closed system for materials. This means that although many of Earth's resources cycle and are renewable, they are limited. New matter will not form and existing matter can become something else but it will not go away.

Let's get talking

Discuss this question with a partner or small group:

Why should we care that Earth is considered a closed system?

Write and draw what you understand about open and closed systems in your Project Notebook.

Explaining Earth's processes

Look at the activity on page 87–89. Work together as a class to read the information on natural processes, and answer the questions about this picture.

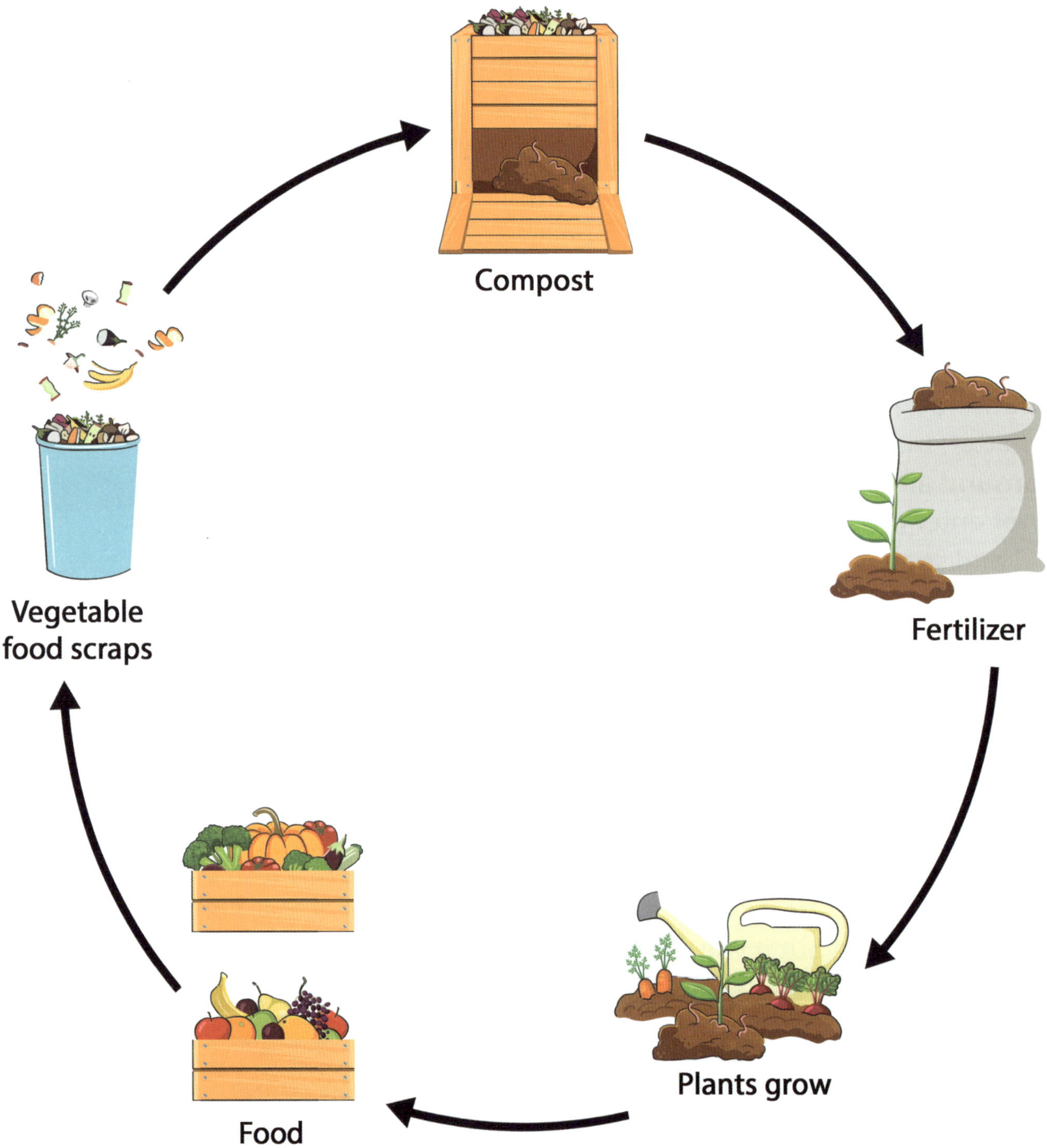

Laws and principles that support life on Earth

Complete the rest of the activity on your own.

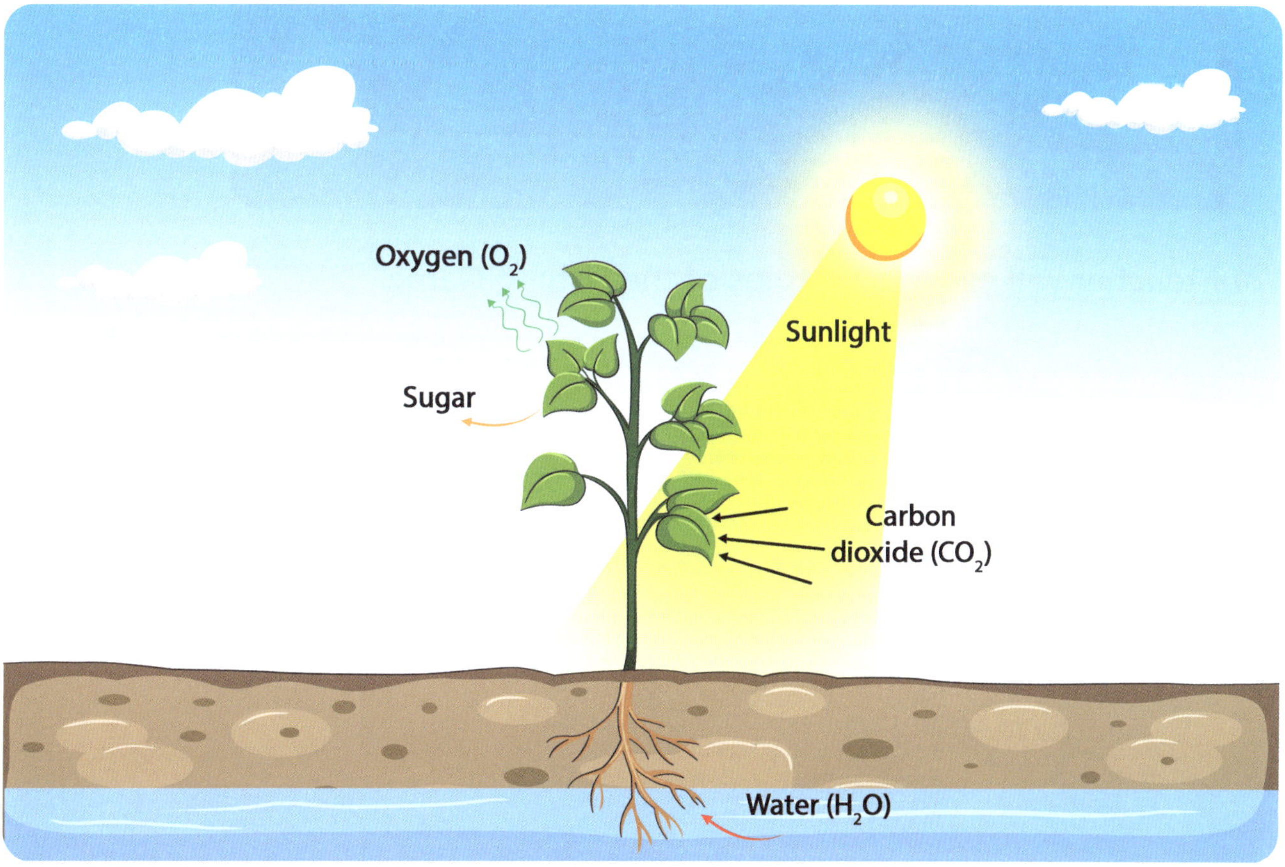

Let's go fishing!

How can we all live well and look after the health of the living systems that we depend on and that depend on us?

Before we try to answer this question, use the activity on page 90–91 and play the Fishing Game.

Your teacher will explain the rules of the Fishing Game.

Carrying capacity

Carrying capacity is the most balanced number of organisms of a particular species that can live indefinitely in a system (given the amount of food, space, and so on).

Think about the results of the Fishing Game. If you who took 'too much', *why* did you do it?

Think about it! There are many reasons why people take more than they need.

It is important to think about our thinking and reasons because the right thinking leads to the right actions.

Answer the following questions in your Project Notebook:

- Why did we run out of fish in one or more of the games?
- What did it take to catch fish without running out of fish?

Exceeding the supply

In the Fishing Game, we saw what happens if we try to have unlimited use of a limited commons (the fish supply) without the agreements and laws to control the activity. The game showed us that this is unsustainable. If we do it, we will have no fish. What can we do?

To answer the question, we need to do the following:

- Do the maths and find out the limits of what we can do without using all of a commons.
- Find out how much of the commons we need, both as a community and as individuals.
- Find solutions and discuss agreements between individuals in the community and between different communities. We need to find a way to have fish in the future!

For example, think about our Fishing Game. What is the greatest number of fish that can be taken out of the sea each round (adding back 25% to the sea) in total?

The answer is four.

How do we make sure that we don't take out more than four fish each round? Think of new rules for the game that we can all agree on.

For example: Take turns not fishing or doing other activities. What are other creative ideas?

Let's get talking

Discuss and share ideas:

- What happens when our demand for resources uses all the supply?
- What natural resources do we use in our community?
- Are any of them in danger from being used too much?

Supply and demand

Read the definitions below.

- **Supply:** the quantity of something that is available for use or to buy, for example, the number of apples that a village produces.
- **Demand:** the quantity of something that people need or want to use or to buy, for example, the number of apples people in the village need or want to eat to have a healthy diet.
- **Carrying capacity:** the quantity of something that the ecosystem can have without creating problems to it or to parts of it, for example, the number of apple trees you can grow in an area without using pesticides or all the water in the river, and at the same time grow other foods people need to live.
- **Replenishment rate**: the amount of time it takes for resources to be restored and renewed: to grow back (plants), to be born and grow up (animals), or to be refilled (water).

Think about what you learned from the Fishing Game and apply these ideas to other examples!

Look at the picture and meaning of overgrazing.

Overgrazing is caused when animals eat all the grass and plants on a piece of land before the plants can grow again.

Results:

- It changes the soil and makes it difficult for plants to grow again.
- It can cause loss of soil, floods, a loss of diversity and plants, and even affects how much rain falls in the area.

Now complete Part 1 of the activity on page 92–93 as a class, and Part 2 on your own.

The future you want

Imagine what you want to eat for lunch tomorrow, and describe it as if it is happening now.

You could say, "I am having lunch."

Or you could say, "I am having a warm stew, full of vegetables, with rice."

The second description creates a positive vision about something you care about.

We can create and shape our preferred futures.

Vision, imagination, and determination are important to creating the future you want.

Practise making a fun vision for what your class will have for lunch tomorrow.

How can we create a vision we all agree on?

The future of your community

Read Kabir and Anika's visions for the future:

In the future that I want, the streets in my neighbourhood have plants and there is no litter. There is a community compost bin where everyone can take their vegetable food scraps, everyone wastes less, and reuses more. – *Kabir, Year 5*

In ten years from now, I hope the air where I live is cleaner. Right now, there is bad air pollution from industry. In the future I want, we have found ways to remove the bad bits from the air, and companies are responsible for producing goods without polluting the air. – *Anika, Year 5*

What do you think your community will be like in the future?

In your Project Notebook, write a statement like Kabir's and Anika's to describe your preferred future for your community.

Share your ideas with a partner or in small groups.

After hearing your classmate's ideas, is there anything that you would like to add to your own statement?

Think about it! What are some things that affect the health of a community?

What are some indicators of a healthy community?

For example:

- resource usage
- conditions of schools, roads, and other public commons
- clean water and air
- amount of green space
- safe streets.

What else?

Flexible thinking

Read the definition of flexible thinking and write your own version in your Project Notebook under the 'My Personal Word Bank' heading.

Flexible thinking is the ability to look at a situation and see it in a different way, or find creative solutions to a problem. It is like a rubber band – you can make it longer without breaking it (if you don't pull it too much!).

Rigid thinking is the opposite of flexible thinking. The person sees only one side of things, does not listen when someone shows them another side and another way of doing things, and does not want to discuss things with people they disagree with. It is like a rock – it changes very slowly or not at all.

Let's get talking

Discuss: How can flexible thinking support growth or change?

Think about it! Think back to Spaceship Earth and the Fishing Game. How did flexible and creative thinking support working together to create solutions?

We know that it is important to think about our thinking. Flexible thinking can help lead us to new ideas or imagine possible scenarios in the right direction of our preferred future!

What if?

Read the following scenario out loud:

More and more children at our school want to join the football team. According to the new rules, only twenty children can be in the team. In some years, there aren't enough children to fill the team but, in our year, more than twenty children joined the team!

What might happen? What are the possible results?

We cannot predict exactly what will happen with certainty, only what might happen if this or that happens.

Scenario planning helps us imagine different kinds of futures that we might experience in different situations. If we study the possible results of many different scenarios, we can often make better decisions.

Work together to complete the scenario planning activity on page 94.

After you complete the activity, share your ideas. How could we use scenario planning to work towards the future we want for our community?

Inventing your future

Go back to the statement about the future you want from Lesson 7.

Take turns to share your statements with the rest of the class and make a note of any similarities in your statements.

Work together to agree a class description of the future you want for your community.

Identify key questions about how to achieve the future you want.

Example: Our vision for the community includes safety for all the people who live here.

Example key question: What could we do to make sure our community is safe over the next twenty years?

Write down a key question in your Project Notebook.

Identify certainties and uncertainties:

Certainties

- People will always want to be safe.
- There are rules in our community to keep us safe.

Uncertainties

- Future population changes, available jobs, and resources
- When current safety issues will be resolved
- What changes people will accept
- What technological solutions will be available

Thrive over time

Read the list of laws and principles from nature again.

Laws and principles from nature

1. Nature uses sunlight and sugar.
2. Nature recycles everything because there is no such place as 'away'.
3. Nature thrives on diversity.
4. Nature uses the power of limits.
5. In nature, everything and everyone is interdependent and interconnected.

Use the following grid to imagine four possible futures for your key question on page 24.

Best-case scenario:	Possible future X:
Possible future Y:	**Worst-case scenario:**

Discuss: What are the positive and negative points of each scenario? How can we thrive over time in each scenario?

Explain how you used the principles from nature to think about the scenarios. Talk about this with a partner.

Complete the activity on page 95, on the key question you developed for your preferred future.

Best-case scenarios

Look at the notes in your Project Notebook on your key question from Lesson 9.

Work in groups to discuss your different scenarios. Remember that each scenario is a possible future for your community!

- **What are the positive and negative points of each scenario?**
- **How can we thrive over time in each scenario?**
- **What similarities are there between the different scenarios?**

Read the following text:

When we think about the future we want, we imagine something that doesn't exist yet. This is known as structural tension. There are two ways to deal with the difference between our current reality and the future we want: accept less than we want (not the best option), or find ways to achieve what we want and work hard to achieve it (best option)!

Let's get talking

- **In your mind, picture your community as it is right now, in your current reality.**
- **How might you get from where you are now to where you want to be (your preferred future)?**
- **What are some differences that exist between your current reality and your preferred future?**

Children invent the future!

Read the following stories from children making a difference.

Words have power

10-year-old Jaysea united the community with her speeches about how the local power station caused asthma. When the community succeeded in shutting down the station, Jaysea concluded that "words have power".

Save tomorrow

After seeing the Young Voices for the Planet films, three 9-year-old girls asked their town hall to change a town law (with full community support!) to allow solar panels on public buildings. They then saved their local woods.

Plant for the planet

As a 9-year-old boy, encouraged by Wangari Maathai, Felix started Plant for the Planet. Now, through his global website, he has planted more than a billion trees in Germany and in other parts of the world.

Now that you have read the stories from the children, complete the activity on page 96. Create a storyboard with drawings, which shows how you might plan for the best-case scenario.

What is sustainability anyway?

Read the definitions below.

Sustain: to provide enough of what somebody or something needs in order to live or exist.

Ability: the fact that somebody or something is able to do something.

Read several definitions of sustainability and then work together as a class to write a definition of sustainability. Create a poster that shows this definition and put it up in the classroom.

"The capability to thrive over time"
– Jaimie P. Cloud

"The possibility that human and other life will flourish on the planet forever"
– John R. Ehrenfeld

"Sustainability is when people get what they want without destroying the world so animals and other people can get what they want and need."
– Thomas, aged 9

"A sustainable society is one that is far-seeing enough, flexible enough, and wise enough not to undermine either its physical or its social systems of support."
– Donella Meadows

Discuss: What helps achieve sustainability?

Some ideas ...

... living within the natural laws and limits that exist on planet Earth

... people's actions or lack of actions

Defining sustainability

Copy and complete the following sentences in your Project Notebook.

- In order for our community to be sustainable, ...
- In a sustainable community, resources are ...

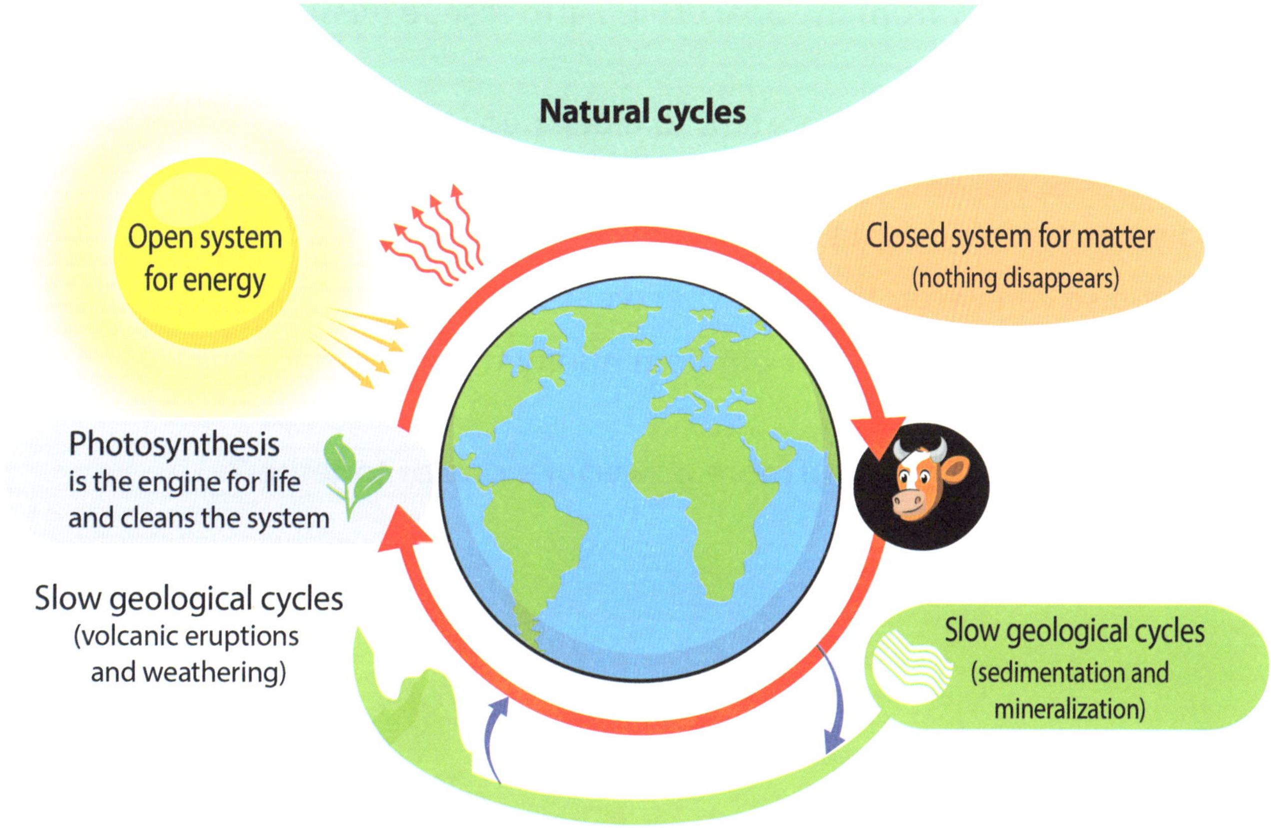

Let's get talking

Look at the diagram above.

Sustainability is the ability of society to continue indefinitely within these cycles.

What does this make you think about Earth? Think about Spaceship Earth. Talk about this question with a partner.

Write a postcard or short letter to share your definition of sustainability with someone in your community.

We invent the future

Share the most interesting part of the project with a partner.

Review the assessment criteria for the learning outcome. Read the 'Extending' criteria.

Return to your crew from the Spaceship Earth rescue mission and share ideas:

- Why do you think it is important to teach people about sustainability?
- How can we use our postcards to teach others?
- What else can we do to share what we learned?
- What is most important for our community to understand?

Discuss: Do you think we are more powerful alone or together? Why?

Answer these questions in your Project Notebook:

Do children have the ability to invent the future? In what ways can we help build the future that we all want? Explain your ideas using examples.

After the project

You have completed your project!

Write and share your ideas to help you remember what we have learned and why it is important.

What are you proud of in this project?

____

____

What skills did you practise in this project?

____

____

Why is sustainability important?

____

____

Draw a picture that shows that we must follow the laws and principles from nature so that we can live well on our Spaceship Earth now and in the future.

Think about what you need to help build the future you want.

Do something good for Earth every day!

2 Contributing to the health of our commons

Contents

Dear Student,

Welcome to your second Sustainability project of the year. Get ready to learn from real-world stories that show us how to protect and care for our commons. You will explore different communities that have worked together to preserve their shared resources, just like you after this project!

You will choose a commons that is important to you and come up with ideas on how to keep it healthy over time. You will create agreements that will help us take responsibility for the effect of our actions.

By the end of this project, you will have a deeper understanding of the commons and their importance, as well as new skills to be sustainability caretakers of your own community.

Have fun exploring and working on your project!

Best wishes,

The Sustainability Team

Learning from Apo Island

Read the Welcome letter on page 33. Share something that interests you about this new project.

What connections can you make to previous Sustainability projects?

Read the following case study.

Apo Island: A fishing success story

In the Philippines, there is a small fishing village called Apo Island. The fishermen there used to catch fish sustainably using traditional methods. Over time, the population got bigger and there was more demand for fish. As the demand grew, things began to change. The fishermen started using harmful methods of fishing, such as dynamite, cyanide (a type of poison), and throwing rocks on the coral reef to make the fish swim away from it into the nets. This led to terrible damage of the coral reef (the habitat) and to taking fish from the sea faster than young fish were being born (overfishing). This caused fish populations to decline which, in turn, led to a lack of food and a lack of jobs for the people in the village.

However, in 1979, a marine scientist suggested the idea of creating a no-fishing sanctuary, a protected area where no fishing was allowed. Apo Island set aside 10 percent of their fishing areas as a no-fishing sanctuary. Families shared responsibility and took turns guarding it. This led to amazing results: nature had time to repair the damage, and the fish and coral started to come back.

Apo Island, the Philippines

A coral reef near the island

Encouraged by their success, the islanders made more rules to protect their fish population. They stopped using harmful fishing methods, banned outsiders from fishing, and worked together to manage their ecosystem. They made more and more people aware of the problems and the solutions, and added the subject of marine ecology in schools. Today, Apo Island has a healthy coral reef, popular eco-tourism, and better jobs for the community. Other villages in the Philippines have learned from Apo Island's success and have created their own marine sanctuaries.

Fishermen's boats on an Apo Island beach

Talk about the following questions:

- Why did the fish population in Apo Island decline?
- How did the decline change the lives of the fishermen and the village?
- What idea did the marine scientist introduce to Apo Island?
- How did it help repair the fish and coral populations?
- How did the islanders work together to protect their fish population?
- What were some of the positive results of their work for both the environment and the community?

Work with a partner. Find at least two ways that the people of Apo Island took responsibility for protecting and caring for their commons. Write a paragraph about your ideas in your Project Notebook.

Our shared languages

Talk about the following questions:

- Can we use too much of an unlimited commons?
- Can we not use enough of an unlimited commons?

What language or languages do you speak?
What languages are spoken in your community?

Reviving the Māori language

Māori refers to the indigenous people of New Zealand, and their language, culture, arts, and traditions.

Traditional Māori wood-carved canoes

When Europeans first arrived in New Zealand, they took control of the country. They imposed their own language, English, and culture on the Māori population. English became the main language of education, government, and communication. This led to a decline in the use of the Māori language among younger people.

Young Māori sisters

The government wanted to prevent the use of the Māori language in schools. Many Māori children were punished for speaking their language at school. Speaking Māori became a negative thing. As a result, many people did not speak the Māori language at all. The language was at risk of becoming extinct, as fewer people were able to speak it easily and well.

In the 1970s, inspired by global civil rights movements, a group of young Māori known as Nga Tamatoa asked for training for teachers to teach the Māori language in schools. This was the beginning of the Māori language revitalization movement.

Since then, there have been more efforts to revitalize the Māori language. The Māori people and the New Zealand government have promoted the use of Māori in schools, media, and public spaces. At sporting events, the national anthem is now sung in both English and Māori.

The language is used in books, songs, movies, and even on street signs. One of the most important actions was the creation of preschools called 'kohanga reo' ('language nests'), where Māori is the only language used and children learn about Māori traditions and values. It became a huge success and led to more children speaking the Māori language.

A sign in Wellington, New Zealand

The movement didn't stop there. In 2013, only 3.7 percent of New Zealanders spoke Māori fluently. In 2021, the number rose to 7.9 percent. The New Zealand government has now set a goal for one million residents to speak basic Māori by 2040.

This united effort by both Māori and non-Māori New Zealanders will ensure that the Māori language and culture stay alive.

Talk about the following questions:

- Why did the Māori language decline?
- What did the Māori people do to revitalize their language?
- What did the government do to protect the language?

Work with a partner to find at least two ways in which the people of New Zealand took responsibility for protecting and caring for their commons. Write a paragraph about your ideas.

Let's get talking

Look at your notes from the two case studies. With a partner, compare the actions taken by the people of Apo Island and the New Zealanders.

- How did each community care for their commons?
- How are their actions similar?

Learning from others

Read the following case study.

How Japan protected its forests

In the early 1600s, Japan had a serious deforestation problem. The Japanese population was growing, and they cut down too many trees to use as fuel or for building without replacing them. They also cut down forests to grow more food.

A historical picture of a cedar tree in Japan

The people who lived in the villages near the forests knew they had to protect the trees and find a better way to use them. So, around 1670, they started cooperating, planting, and managing the forests together. Woodsmen and government officials worked together to develop new and better ways to grow and care for trees. This included new methods for producing seed, planting tree cuttings, and thinning out the trees. The thinning out meant cutting down only some of the trees to leave more light, water, and food for the other trees.

Japan has many ancient forests.

Cedar forests were particularly important, as cedar is a high-quality wood. People created a method of growing new cedar trees using an older tree as a platform. They planted the new trees on top of the old one, and when they needed wood, they cut just the new ones at the top, not the entire tree. This left the base and roots structure perfectly healthy. The new parts of the cedar could be cut every 20 years, which is far earlier than with other methods, so the method became very popular. It is called 'daisugi'. Experts wrote books about these methods, and travelled around to teach people in different areas how to do it.

A Japanese cedar forest

They also made special rules like 'yamawari', which allowed families to share forest land. People were allowed to rent the land for a long time, and shared the wood that they collected. This all helped the villagers cooperate to take care of the trees and use them well.

Over time, Japan's forests grew back and became healthy again. They became a key resource for the country's development. Japan's forests have faced new challenges over the years, but together, the government and the villagers kept adapting and finding solutions. They learned that taking care of their natural resources was very important for their future, and so made sure they used the forests sustainably.

With a partner or small group, read the case study. Think about the following questions together. Write your answers in your Project Notebook.

- How did the need for wood change as Japan's population grew?
- Why did the situation become difficult?
- What did the people who lived near the forests do?
- What new methods and agreements did they develop?

Let's get talking

Pair up with another group to discuss the question:

What can we learn from Japan's forest story about the importance of taking care of our commons and adapting to changes?

Then complete the activity on page 97 on your own.

We are all connected

We all depend on each other and on Earth's living systems. Think of a choice you could make, or an action you could take, in your community that would have a positive impact on our global commons. Share your thoughts with your class.

Local and global commons

We are all connected, so even small actions in a local commons can affect a global commons. We should always think about what these connections are.

For example, let's think about a local commons, for example pollinators such as bees, butterflies, and other insects, and a global commons, such as air.

How are they connected?

Many plants need pollinators to transfer pollen from one flower to another. This allows the plants to produce seeds and fruits. Air naturally contains oxygen and carbon dioxide, but too much carbon dioxide pollutes the air.

People and animals need oxygen to live and when they breathe, they produce carbon dioxide.

Trees and plants do the opposite: they use energy from the sun, water, and carbon dioxide to produce food and oxygen. This process is called photosynthesis.

So trees and plants reduce the amount of carbon dioxide in the air and increase the amount of oxygen.

Without pollinators, trees and plants can't produce seeds, so they can't produce new plants, so they can't help maintain air quality.

Work with a partner or small group to complete the activity on page 98.

KEY ACTIONS

Work together to create a class list of key actions that can have a positive impact on the health of our commons.

Creating a class trust tree

How is trust important in building strong relationships? Share your ideas with the class.

On a small piece of paper, write down one action or behaviour that helps build and maintain trust in your community. For example, 'Listening to others'. Stick your paper on the branches of a class trust tree.

Read the ideas of others. Decorate the class trust tree.

Read the two possible scenarios for the commons of a lake in the centre of a community on page 43.

Remember that the right thinking leads to the right actions.

How to keep our commons healthy

Scenario 1: We are all responsible

Community members love and care for their local environment. They understand that their actions directly affect the health of the lake. Every weekend, people visit the lake to have picnics and enjoy the place. They make sure they pick up their rubbish, avoid using harmful chemicals, and always treat the lake with care. People who enjoy fishing follow the rules for how many fish they are allowed and during what seasons they can fish.

As the years pass, the lake and the area around it remain full of life: the water is clean, fish swim in it, birds sing, and trees and flowers grow around it.

Scenario 2: No one is responsible

Community members do not take care of their environment. People visit the lake and leave their rubbish behind, thinking someone else will pick it up. Factories near the lake release harmful chemicals into the water without considering the consequences. The lake's health begins to decline as rubbish starts to pile up and fish populations decline. Algae spread over the surface of the water. This is harmful to the lake because algae use up a lot of the oxygen that the fish and other underwater living things need.

Over time, the lake's water turns dirty and dark. It starts to smell bad. The ecosystem breaks, and nobody goes to the lake. People realize too late the consequences of not caring about the lake. Local wildlife suffers. The lack of responsibility leads to the decline of the health of the lake, the people, and the environment.

Let's get talking

Discuss this question as a class: What thoughts, behaviours, and actions contributed to the outcomes in each possible scenario?

Work on your own to complete the activity on page 99–100. Then add to the class list of key actions from the previous lesson.

The Commons Clean-up Team

Look at the playscript that your teacher gives you. Take turns playing different roles in the play. Practise the lines and set up the scenes to bring 'The Commons Clean-up Team' to life.

Emma Zoheb Mia Liam Noah Teacher

Community awareness

Read the definition of community awareness below.

Awareness means knowing that something exists and is important.

When a community pays attention to what's going on around them and care about what happens, we have community awareness. It is an example of an invisible commons.

When we all understand a problem, and each other, we can work together to find solutions.

We can use our different skills, knowledge, and resources to make things better.

Talk about the following questions as a class:

- How was the lack of community awareness a cause of the unhealthy state of the school commons in the play?
- What could happen once everyone understands the problem and cares about solving it?

Describe different ways you can raise community awareness. Write your ideas in your Project Notebook.

Commons challenges

Look at the picture of a public library. Work with a partner to note the problems. Discuss ideas for how to improve the health of this commons. Use your class list of key actions. Write down your thoughts in your Project Notebook.

Read each of the scenarios on page 47. Complete the Let's get talking activity, then complete the activity on page 101–102.

Let's get talking

Discuss these questions as a class.

- Why is it important to take care of the commons in your school?
- How can your actions help prevent challenges and keep the commons healthy?
- What role does everyone in the school community play in taking care of the commons?

Then think about the following questions. Write your answers in your Project Notebook.

- Which of the commons in our school need more awareness or could benefit from our help?
- What are the challenges of these commons?
- What is causing this to happen?
- What can we do about it?

Scenario 1: The school garden

The school garden used to be colourful and healthy. Students and teachers worked together to grow flowers, herbs, and vegetables here. But recently the garden hasn't been very healthy. Some plants are drying out, and weeds are everywhere. It looks like people have forgotten to water and care for the garden.

Scenario 2: The school library

The school library was a great place to study and to find interesting books. However, things have changed. Books are left on the floor, pages are torn, and the library is becoming noisier.

Scenario 3: The school playground

The school playground used to be a fun place where students played games, played on the swings, and enjoyed their breaks. But recently, there have been some problems. There is now more rubbish on the ground and some play equipment is broken. In addition, some students are not treating their classmates kindly during games. They make others feel unhappy or unsafe.

Scenario 4: The school pavements

The pavements near school used to be in very good condition. Students used them to walk and ride their bicycles to school safely. But recently there have been some problems. The pavements have started to break, making it difficult for students to use them without falling. Some parts of the pavements are higher than the rest, making it hard for people using wheelchairs to move around easily.

The sound of our school

Check the noise level in the shared areas of your school. This will help you to discover the health of this invisible commons.

What shows that this commons is healthy? For example, are you able to hear conversations clearly, or do you have to shout to communicate? What other indicators can you look for to measure the health of the noise commons?

Work in groups. Go to your assigned shared area of the school. Take notes in your Project Notebook.

- What activities take place here?
- How many people are present at the time of your observation?
- What sounds and noise do you hear? What is making the noise?
- What level of noise do you think is OK for this area?
- Use colours to show the health of the noise level: red = extremely noisy, yellow = very noisy, green = OK. Explain your decision.

red yellow green

Return to your classroom and share your findings. Discuss what you think is a healthy noise level for each area and why.

Think of ideas for maintaining or improving the noise health in different areas of the school.

Improving unhealthy commons

Look again at your class list of key actions, the commons how-to guide activity, and the activity for Lesson 7.

In your Project Notebook, write a paragraph explaining what it takes to care for a commons over time and how to improve unhealthy commons. Include specific examples from the case studies and scenarios studied. Use the pictures on this page to help you think.

Hard to breathe

What do you already know about air pollution and its effects?
What happens if we breathe dirty air?

Follow along with the pictures as you listen to the story.

As a class, talk about the following questions:

- What activities does Noor notice that can pollute the air?
- Why do you think so many places around the world experience air pollution problems?

Care for the air

Talk with a partner:

- Is air a resource that we all need?
- Is air a resource that we all share?
- Whose responsibility is it to take care of our air and make sure it is clean?

Measuring air quality

Search online for a 'real-time air quality index'. Use it to find the air quality of your local area. Record your findings on the activity on page 103–104. Then, as a class or in small groups, discuss and write the answers to the questions.

Air Quality Index (AQI) values	Level of health concern	Air quality description
When the AQI is …	… the air quality is …	… which means that …
Low	Good	… the air quality is good for everyone.
Medium	Moderate	… the air quality is almost good.
Medium/High	Unhealthy for vulnerable groups	… the air quality is OK for most, but unhealthy for vulnerable persons, such as the very young, the old, or those with health conditions such as asthma.
High	Unhealthy	… everyone begins to experience negative health effects.
Very high	Very unhealthy	… the entire population is likely to be affected.
Extremely high	Hazardous	… this is a health emergency! Everyone is likely to experience serious health effects.

State of the commons

In this project, you have explored many different local and global commons:

- Fish populations and coral reefs
- Languages
- Forests
- Trust
- Community awareness
- Noise at our school
- Air

Which commons do you want to focus on as a class? Work together as a class to choose a commons. What are the key functions of this commons?

Let's get talking

Talk about the question as a class: What is it about the commons that you are focusing on that is so important to protecting the planet or improving our quality of life?

Now talk with a partner:

- Describe the current problems with this commons.
- In what ways is the health of the commons you have chosen in danger?
- Who or what is causing the problems?
- How do you know?

How are you going to measure the health of your chosen commons?

Your teacher will give you some examples of indicators that can be used to measure the health of various commons. You are going to develop a set of indicators that you can use to measure the health of your chosen commons over time.

Measuring the health

You will first need to decide what questions to ask and research for your specific commons. For example:

The school library

Goal: To understand how students in our school use the library

Research questions:

- How many students use the library daily/weekly/monthly? How does this compare with the total number of students in the school?
- What is available for students to use in the library? Is there a large variety of books? Are there computers? Is there internet access?
- How often are books replaced or new books added?
- What is the library like inside? Is the lighting strong and bright? Is there good ventilation? Are there tables and chairs to work at?
- How do students treat the library? Is it quiet? Is it clean? How well is it looked after?

Think about the commons that your class chose. Work in small groups to write up to five of the most important research questions you can think of.

Then spend some time thinking of specific ways that you could find out the answers to your questions. For the above example, you could interview your school librarian, create a questionnaire for students in your school about how they use the library, and visit the library to observe how it is used.

Finally, use your questions and research methods to develop up to ten possible indicators for your chosen commons.

Example indicators for the school library:

- The number of people who use the library
- The type of available resources (books, digital materials)
- The condition of the resources
- How well the library is looked after and maintained
- Noise levels, lighting, and ventilation
- The range of activities that take place in the library

Asking questions and doing research helps us to come up with creative solutions and make agreements.

Children's Clean Air Manifesto

A manifesto is a written statement that describes the views of the person or group who write it. It is usually shared publicly.

Read the following manifesto written by a group of children.

Children's Clean Air Manifesto

We, the children of the world, declare our right to breathe clean and fresh air.

We believe:

- Clean air is our right, just like clean water and healthy food.
- Trees and plants help to keep the air clean. We promise to protect them as they protect us.
- Cars can be cleaner: we ask adults to make cars that don't pollute the air. Electric and solar-powered cars can be our future.
- No more smoke: Smoking damages our lungs and the air.
- Clean energy, please: We want energy that comes from wind, sun, and waves. These are clean and won't make our air dirty.
- We will buy fewer things, reuse them, and recycle what we can. Less waste means cleaner air.
- We will tell adults to protect our air and fight against pollution. We won't be silent, because our voices matter.
- We will learn more about clean air and share our knowledge with friends, family, and everyone we meet.

We promise to care for our air today and every day for a cleaner, healthier world.

Let's get talking

Discuss the questions:

- **What do you think led the children to write this manifesto?**
- **Who do you think it is for?**

Our manifesto

A manifesto is a great tool to produce change. Your ideas can make a difference in how people care for the commons you care for.

Follow the ideas below to develop a class manifesto for the commons. Use the activity on page 105 to collaborate.

Developing your manifesto

- ✓ Set clear goals: Decide what you want to achieve for this commons. (For example, if it's a local park, your goal might be to reduce littering and make it more beautiful.)
- ✓ Write down specific actions you and others can take to achieve these goals. These should be practical and achievable.
- ✓ Include everyone: Remember that a manifesto is a statement for everyone. Think about how people of different ages, backgrounds, and abilities can contribute.
- ✓ Use strong language and words that will make people want to join your work.
- ✓ Keep it positive: Focus on what you want to achieve rather than what you want to avoid.
- ✓ Provide reasons: Explain why each action is important. Share facts, stories, or examples that support your ideas.

Share your learning!

Care for our Commons Day!

Ideas for sharing your manifesto:

- Post the manifesto on the wall, present it at a community event, distribute copies, and ask an adult to share it on the internet to reach a wider audience.
- Encourage people to share with others and keep spreading the word!

Discuss what was achieved during the 'Care for our Commons Day'.

How did we help change the thinking and behaviours of members of our community to support the health of our commons?

After the project

You have completed your project!

Write and share your ideas to help you remember what we have learned and why it is important.

What are you most proud of in this project?

____

____

What skills did you practise during this project?

____

____

Why is it important to work for the health of our commons?

____

____

Draw a picture that reminds others that we need to protect and care for our commons.

Think about what you need to do to achieve your goal.

Do one good thing for Earth every day!

3 Taking inspiration from nature

Contents

Dear Student,

Welcome to your third and final Sustainability project of the year. Get ready to use nature as a source of ideas.

This project is about respecting and learning from the world around us. Throughout the project, we will use creative thinking inspired by nature – biomimicry – to find solutions to problems.

You will present recommendations about how to reduce and eliminate waste. You will show how everything is connected and how these natural systems help us to live well over time. We will also continue to explore how we depend on plants and animals. You will also become teachers! You will work together to create a learning experience for younger students, helping them to understand the idea of interdependence.

So, get ready to explore, design, recommend, and teach. We can't wait to see what amazing things you will achieve.

Have fun exploring and working on your project!

Best wishes,

The Sustainability Team

Our new project

Read the Welcome letter and set up your Project Notebook for your new project.

Share what interests you about this new project with a partner.

People have often found solutions to human problems by studying nature and copying natural systems. This strategy is called biomimicry.

Read these examples of how people learned from nature.

Velcro is used to fasten clothes, shoes, and many other things. It was invented in 1941 when a Swiss man named George de Mestral looked closely at the burdock seeds that he found in his dog's fur after a walk. Like the seed, Velcro has tiny hooks that stick to the loops in fabric.

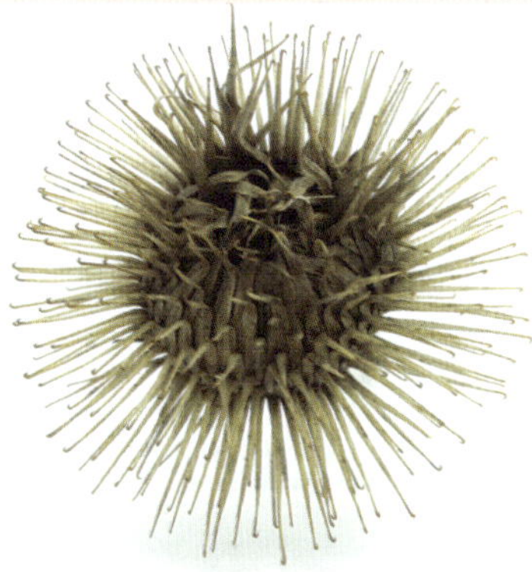

Termites build their homes in tall structures called mounds. These mounds are very strong, but also have walls with lots of small holes that let air in and keep the whole mound cool. This technology can be used to keep buildings cool.

What if?

Discuss these questions as a class:

- How can we work well with nature?
- What could we do differently in how we live in and with nature?
- What can we learn from the way nature and life work?
- What would happen if everyone started thinking about nature as a place to learn ideas?

Share an example with the class of a time of when you worked with a partner or a group. How did your pair or group achieve your goal?

Nature can inspire us. When we work well with nature, we can give back to nature and take care of the world around us.

What have you learned from nature? Give one example. Write your answer in your Project Notebook and add drawings. Share your answer with the class.

How do you see nature?

Read the poems below to see how writers celebrate nature through poetry. After reading them, share your favourite lines and why you chose them.

Seeds

by Hilda I. Rostron

Seeds that twist and seeds that twirl
Seeds with wings which spin and whirl;
Seeds that float on thistledown
Seeds in coats of glossy brown;
Seeds that burst with popping sound
From their pods to reach the ground;
Seeds with hooks that clutch and cling
Seeds I plant for flowers next spring.

Without any water

by Tony Mitton

Without any water
there wouldn't be drinks.
There wouldn't be washing
and there wouldn't be sinks.
There wouldn't be rivers
and there wouldn't be seas.
There wouldn't be water
for plants and trees.
Without any water,
without a drop,
there would be no life
and the world would stop.

Writing nature poems

Nature is all around us – it is the air we breathe, the animals and plants that live and grow in our area, it's even in the cities we have built on top of the earth.

Reflection exercise

Sight: Describe an image of nature that you have seen or imagined.

Sound: Remember a sound you heard in nature that you enjoyed.

Touch: Remember a natural object you touched and describe how it felt.

Smell: Remember a nice smell from nature.

Taste: Think about a taste that reminds you of nature.

You are going to write an original poem about nature.

Choose something from nature that you love, such as a specific plant, animal, place, or natural event (such as a storm). Use language that describes it and your feelings.

Here are some more ideas to help you:

- A sensory poem: what do you see, touch, hear, smell, and feel when you are in nature?
- A poem about feelings: how does being in nature make you feel? Is it calming, exciting, mysterious, or something else?
- A poem about a special moment: do you have a special memory from nature? For example a walk, a picnic, or seeing a rainbow.
- A poem about protecting nature: why is it important to look after the natural world?

Remember, there is no right or wrong way to write a nature poem.

Share your poems. Talk about the ways that we learn from nature.

Undoing the knot

Your teacher will put you into groups.

Choose two students from your group. They should move away and turn around with their backs to the group, so that they cannot see what happens.

The rest of the group stands in a circle, holding hands. Form a knot by walking between other people, in front of them, and going under locked hands. You must keep holding hands while you are making the knot.

Now the two students must work together and give instructions to the classmates in the knot, to find a way to untangle it and form the circle again.

If needed, you can help the two students by giving them suggestions.

When you have finished, talk about the following questions as a group:

Let's get talking

- How did you work together to find the solution?
- Did everyone have a chance to share their suggestions?
- What worked well? What could you do better?

The point of many games is to have just one person or team as the winner. In this activity, the goal is to solve a problem that can be solved only if you work together, and respect and support each other. When you have answered the questions, try the activity again.

Treating nature with respect

Talk about these questions as a class:

Let's get talking

- How do you show respect to your teacher?
- How do you show respect to your friends and classmates?
- How do you show respect to yourself?

Just like people, we need to treat nature with respect. In what ways can we respect nature? Discuss this question with a partner, then share your answers with the class.

Did you include any of the following in your answers?

- We can be kind to living things, like plants and animals.
- We can look after our water and not waste it.
- We can make sure that when we spend time outside, we do not leave rubbish behind. We can sort our rubbish and put it in the correct bins.
- We can pick up litter that we see in public spaces, like our school and our local park.
- We can share what we know with others.

After the discussion, write notes on this question on your own in your Project Notebook:
How can I be a partner to nature?

Principles of biomimicry

Read the biomimicry principles below to learn more about biomimicry.

Organisms and ecosystems:

- adapt to changes in their environment
- use energy and materials efficiently
- have interdependent relationships within their living systems
- improve living systems rather than harm them
- grow and develop all the time.

Look at the picture of the oak tree and read the text.

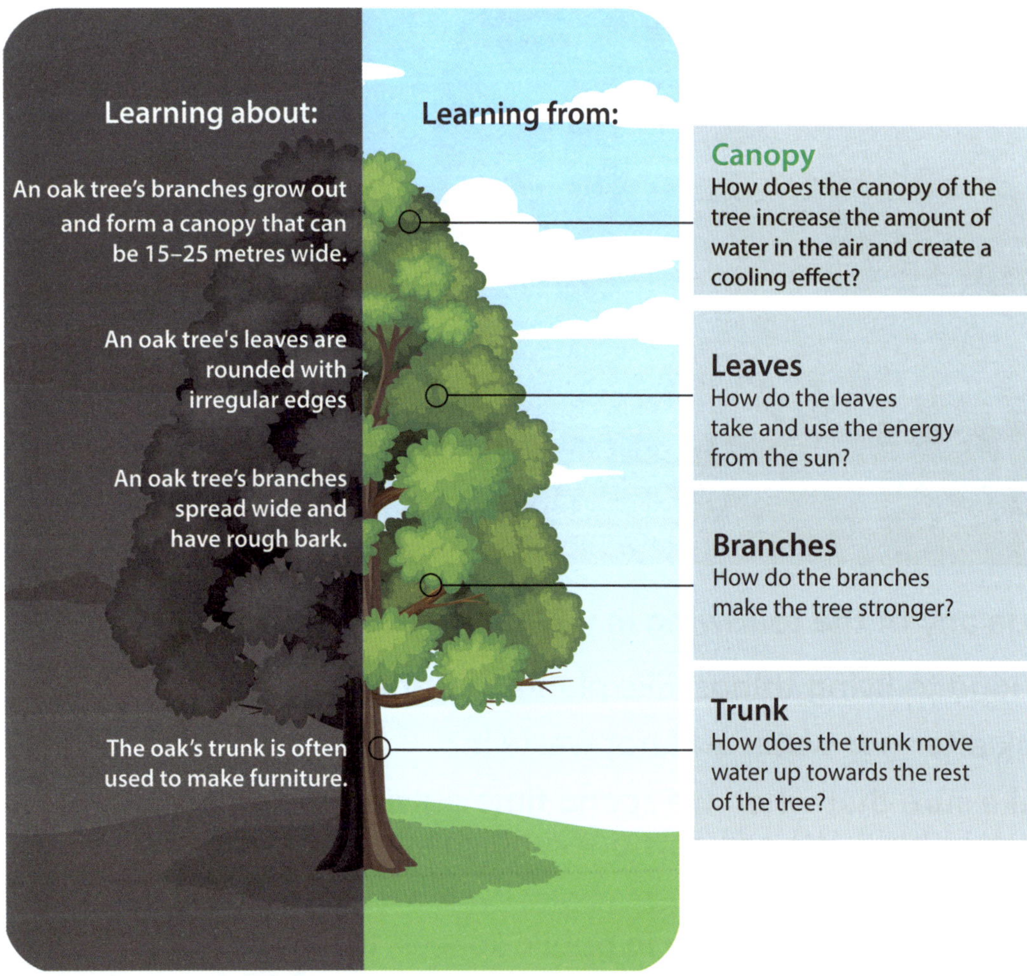

Work with a partner. Think about a living thing from nature, either a plant or an animal. What are the features that help it to live and thrive? Make notes in your Project Notebook.

Design challenge

Identify a problem in your life and community. Think about the biomimicry principles and find a solution that does not create waste. What does your solution need to do? What limits are there?

Try thinking of the problem you want to solve as a question that begins with: "How could we ... ?" For example:

- How could we make sure everybody has enough food and no food is wasted? (Goal: Stop food waste.)
- How could we stop paper/plastic waste? (Goal: Stop paper/ plastic waste.)
- How could we make shoes/backpacks/pens and pencils with no waste? (Goal: Stop shoe/textile/stationery waste.)

Guidelines

Step
1. Understand the challenge. What problem are you trying to solve? What are the limits?
2. Look for solutions in nature. Think about what different living things do that can be useful to copy.
3. Look for similarities in use, structure, or behaviour. For example, if you are designing a water filtration system, look at how plants filter water through their roots.
4. Use design principles. What does your solution need to be like? Efficient, adaptable, resilient? Think about how living things achieve their goals with the best use of energy, without waste, or impact on the environment.
5. Use the biomimicry principles to make your design. Think about how you can copy nature's solutions. For example: • look at the strength and flexibility of spider silk or bamboo for lightweight and durable structures • learn from lotus leaves or shark skin for self-cleaning surfaces • research how birds save energy while flying.

You will continue to work on your design over the next two lessons.

Look to nature

The following example is a real design that students just like you sent to the Biomimicry Institute's Youth Design Challenge.

MorphoBrick

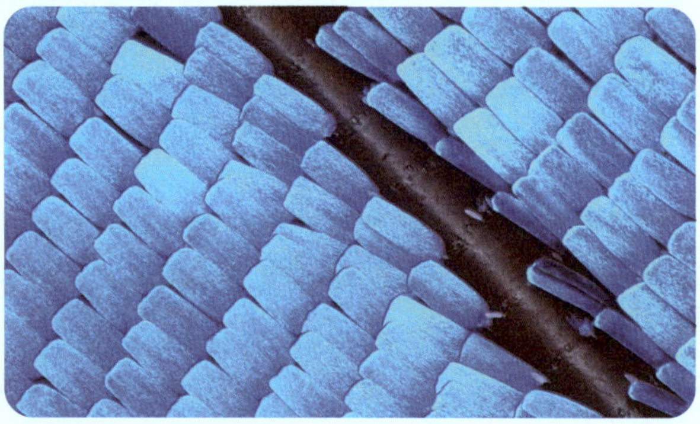

Students learned in school that the heating and cooling systems used in buildings around the world create large amounts of harmful gases. Their goal was to reduce the amount of non-renewable materials that we burn for heating. They thought the solution could be buildings that can control their inside temperature.

The team developed an idea for a new type of brick that can change its colour and surface to either absorb heat or reflect heat, depending on the temperature outside. The brick has a unique four-layer structure that would make buildings that use it more energy-efficient.

The students got the idea from the Morpho butterfly's wings. The wings' scale-like structure reflects light waves to produce bright colours, which the butterflies use for camouflage (to hide from predators), to control their temperature (stay cool or warm), and to communicate with other butterflies.

Share your idea from Lesson 4 with a partner and ask for feedback. Review your design and make any changes or improvements. Make notes in your Project Notebook.

Imagining solutions

Begin the activity on page 106–107 for this lesson. You will complete it in Lesson 6. You can work on your own, in pairs, or in small groups. Use the example below and on page 68 to guide your work.

The following example is based on a design that a group of students from London, England developed in the Biomimicry Institute's Youth Design Challenge.

Goal:

The goal of their design is to find a way to remove fallen branches and plants from railways without cutting down trees.

Research notes:

In what ways do living things get clean? In what ways do living things know there is an object in their way? How do they clear (remove) it?

- Remora fish attach to bigger fish using a special type of fin. This fin also allows them to clean the bigger fish.
- Whales separate their food from seawater using their baleen, a type of sieve in their mouths.
- Smalltooth sawfish have a saw-like snout that they use to scrape the seabed for food.

Possible solutions:

- A clearing tool that attaches to the front of the train
- Sweeping tools or bristle (brush) cleaners
- A grate to clear leaves and debris from rails while the train is moving

Discuss your design plans with your classmates to give and receive helpful and specific feedback. Remember to be kind when you give your feedback.

Bring your design to life

Explore the different materials you might use to create a prototype of your design. A prototype is the first model of a design. It allows you to see if your design will work in real life.

To produce your prototype, you can:

- make it with recycled materials such as cardboard, fabric, or plastic
- design it on your computer
- draw it to scale, creating a detailed illustration.

Complete the activity from Lesson 5.

Who needs to see our designs?

Read about the Biomimicry Youth Design Challenge.

SUSTAINABLE DEVELOPMENT GOALS

The Sustainable Development Goals (SDGs) are 17 global goals created by the United Nations to promote wellbeing while protecting the planet. They are about the global challenges we face, including those related to poverty, climate, environmental damage, and peace – and recognize that all of these goals are interconnected. Together, they represent a shared vision that people around the world are using to work together towards a sustainable future.

In order for us to achieve the SDGs, the systems people build must work together with the systems of the natural world. Nature is one of the best models we have for a sustainable way of living, and biomimicry provides a way of finding the solutions we need. Living things and ecosystems offer great inspiration and strategies that we can copy and apply to both local and global issues in areas like energy, water, transportation, buildings, food systems, health, and more.

You are challenged to explore the wonders of the natural world and create a new idea that helps with one or more of the United Nations SDGs by solving a problem of your choice.

Learn more and register at youthchallenge.biomimicry.org.

Let's get talking

Discuss these questions with a partner:

- Why is it important to share our original designs and ways of thinking with others?
- How has this design process helped us to better understand and connect to nature?

Would you be interested in entering your design in this challenge?

How else could you share your ideas and solutions with others?

Materials recovery

A policy is an agreed plan of action developed by the leaders of, for example, a country, a business, or a school. Read the following case study.

E-waste materials recovery in Taiwan

In the 1970s and 1980s, it was common for people in Taiwan to dump solid waste, such as old electrical equipment, in rivers and on streets. In 1997, Taiwan began its '4-in-1 Recycling Programme', which aimed to reduce solid waste, increase recycling, and make the recycling industry more efficient and safer.

Under the 4-in-1 Programme, manufacturers and importers of new goods now had to pay to help with the costs of recycling the goods when they were no longer used. As a result, waste quantities in Taiwan have decreased from 1.14 kg per person per day in 1997 to 0.4 kg per person per day in 2011. The 4-in-1 Programme also led to the creation of Taiwan's recycling sector, and in particular, the waste electrical and electronic equipment (WEEE) recycling sector. By 2011, there were 19 official recycling facilities in Taiwan.

Taiwan's recycling rate of 50% or more for WEEE items is equal to or higher than the recycling rates of countries such as Japan and Korea, and twice as high as the estimated 25% WEEE recycling rate in the United States.

Let's get talking

Discuss as a class: What do you think were some of the policy recommendations that were made to the government?

Materials recovery is a process during which waste is sorted and separated into all the materials that we can recycle and reuse. If you can, find out about your local materials recovery systems and policies.

Work in small groups to identify some challenges that are limiting waste reduction in your local area.

Read the examples below.

Example 1

In December 2023, the United States government produced the 'Draft National Strategy for Reducing Food Loss and Waste and Recycling Organics'. This strategy is one of a few strategies that have the following goals:

- work towards achieving a circular economy
- change policy to stop food waste
- increase the amount of organic material that is recycled.

This strategy would reward people and manufacturers to stop food waste and increase their recycling.

Example 2

Germany is one of the world's leaders in sustainable waste management. The country has mandatory waste sorting policies, which have greatly improved its waste management and increased its recycling rates. Germany agreed three major policies to ensure that manufacturers and private industries, not just consumers, are also responsible for managing waste and paying for the costs.

Example 3

Japan's 'Extended Producer Responsibility' policies require manufacturers to take responsibility for the entire life cycle of their products, including collection and recycling, reducing waste, and promoting sustainable practices.

With your group, think of policy recommendations for materials recovery for the challenges you have identified.

Write down your ideas in your Project Notebook. Include the reasons why you are proposing the policy and the expected impact. Who or what could benefit?

Share your group's policy recommendations with the class.

Discuss similarities and add ideas shared by others to your notes.

Communicate to make change

Look again at your policy recommendations from Lesson 7. Discuss any further ideas or questions before you continue with the lesson. Then read the example policy recommendation letter.

Dear [Policy Makers],

We are a group of students interested in exploring creative ways to reduce and eliminate waste. We have written some policy recommendations that we believe can make a lasting impact on our local materials recovery practices. We are excited to share our ideas with you.

1. Start an 'Eco-Educators Programme' in local schools.

This programme aims to empower students with knowledge and skills about waste reduction, recycling, and responsible consumption. By including these lessons in school programmes, we believe students will be able to promote sustainability, influencing their families and the wider community.

Key actions:

- Include waste reduction and recycling lessons in the school curriculum and encourage students to take responsibility for their actions.
- Encourage students to share their knowledge with family and friends, creating a ripple effect of sustainable practices.

2. Put community recycling points in public spaces.

These points would make recycling easier for the community. It would also encourage everyone to make sustainable choices. Bins with correct labels would help people to separate recyclables from general waste and achieve higher recycling rates in our community.

Key actions

- Build accessible recycling points in parks, shopping areas, and community centres.
- Clearly label bins so that people place the correct waste in the correct bin.
- Work with local businesses and organizations to sponsor and maintain these recycling points.

We believe that these policy recommendations can help to build a sustainable community. Thank you for considering our ideas.

Making our recommendations public

Discuss the the question below in small groups, then share ideas with the whole class.

Let's get talking

What did you find most effective about the letter?

Choose one or two of the best ideas for policy recommendations to develop as a class. Describe the key points for the recommendations in your Project Notebook.

Make a plan to share your policy recommendations. For example, you could do one or more of the following:

- Attend a public meeting.
- Invite members of the local waste management policy makers, local politicians, or representatives of the community to a presentation at your school.
- Arrange a presentation with local leaders at a local community centre.
- Write a letter to local politicians.

Decide on the specific audience for your policy recommendations. What is their role or title? What is an appropriate written or spoken greeting? How will the audience affect your presentation or letter?

Prepare your presentations. You could also include visual or other elements (such as photographs) to make your recommendations more effective.

If you are going to give a presentation, practise it. Give and receive feedback about how best to present to a public audience. Listen carefully and respectfully to suggestions from your group members, and include their feedback in your presentation.

Making change

Read about these young people who work to make changes to policy in organizations and their countries.

Anjali Sharma is a climate activist from Melbourne, Australia, a country in which climate change has had serious consequences. Anjali was part of a group of teenagers who asked a judge to stop the government from starting a new fossil fuel project in Australia. In 2021, a judge agreed with her and ruled that the Minister for the Environment had a duty not to harm Australian children or their future.

Vanessa Nakate is a climate activist from Kampala, Uganda. She has used letters, lectures, articles, and social media to bring attention to a wide range of climate issues, including the rise of global temperatures, and the harmful effects of human activity on the planet's rainforests. As a member of various councils and groups, she is also able to influence policy in organizations.

Saoirse Exton began her climate activism at age 13 in her hometown of Limerick, Ireland. She believes that traditional knowledge and storytelling can give people the tools to protect Earth and encourage them to do it. In 2023, Saoirse became the youngest-ever member of the United Nations (UN) Secretary-General's Youth Advisory Group (YAG) on Climate Change. As part of this group, she represents the way young people think, and gives recommendations and solutions to the UN Secretary-General.

Moving towards our goals

Discuss the importance of sharing ideas for positive change and the impact your policy recommendations might have.

What is your goal? What changes do you need to make to meet this goal?

It's now policy presentation day! Present your waste reduction policy recommendations to your audience. Ask for questions and feedback at the end.

After you have presented, discuss how your presentation went as a class.

Publish and share!

Talk about this question: How can we responsibly use online platforms to support working together at a global level?

Contribute to or create an online platform (for example, a blog, your school's website, a local news outlet website) to share your policy recommendations with a wider audience.

Did you know that there is a Youth Advisory Group on Climate Change?

The UN Secretary-General's Youth Advisory Group on Climate Change provides advice for climate action, and offers different types of ideas and specific recommendations.

The UN supports young people all over the world who are taking action in support of a healthy, sustainable future for all.

Find out more about how to get involved!

Review interdependence

Interdependence is the relationship between two or more species that depend on each other to survive.

We are interdependent with, and dependent on, our natural resources and commons.

Talk about this question with a partner: How does thinking about interdependence affect the way we think and act? Think about reciprocity.

A red-billed oxpecker eats insects off a cape buffalo – the buffalo is free from annoying insects, and the bird gets food at the same time. This is an example of one of the many different relationships in nature.

All of our food comes from nature. Think about all the different plants we can eat.

Creative ways to teach

Let's get talking

Talk about the question in pairs or small groups:

Why is it important for everyone to know about interdependence?

Make a web together!

- Sit in a circle.
- One student represents the sun. This student holds a ball of string or wool.
- Everyone else can choose a plant, animal, or other element (such as air or rocks) they want to represent in the circle.
- The students who have a direct connection to the sun raise their hand.
- The sun chooses a student who has their hand raised to pass the ball of string to, while holding onto one end.
- The student with the ball explains what they are and the connection they have to the sun.
- The process then continues, with students raising their hands if there is a connection to the previous student. Each student passes the ball and holds on to the string as it is passed and as connections begin to weave into a web.

Talk about these questions as a class:

- What would happen if one part of the web changes?
- What does this make you think about interdependence?

You will now be responsible for teaching younger students what interdependence means!

What are some of the ways that we learn about big ideas in sustainability and other subjects? What are some creative ways we could teach interdependence to younger students? Think of ideas as a class.

Practise your lesson

As the 'teacher', your job is to make sure your students enjoy the learning and have fun.

Discuss and share advice and other ideas to make this a positive learning experience for everyone. For example, try to learn the names of your 'students' and encourage everyone to participate.

At the end of the learning experience, it is important to reflect on what the younger students learned about interdependence from your lesson. Make sure your lesson includes a way to measure what they have learned. For example, this could be a brief discussion, a drawing, or a written response.

Prepare any materials needed for your lesson.

Work with a small group to practise being the teacher, swapping roles to also act as the students for each other.

Provide kind, helpful, and specific feedback.

Helping with learning

You have practised and prepared materials. You are now ready to teach!

Teaching tips:

- Introduce yourself and explain the learning objective.
- Use clear, understandable language.
- Encourage participation and questions.
- Be patient, kind, and supportive.
- Use visual aids and interactive elements or games.
- Make sure that there is a positive and inclusive atmosphere.
- Check for understanding.
- Have fun!

What did the younger students learn?

Review the student work or discussion notes you collected from the younger students during the lesson.

Did the younger students meet the learning objective from your lesson? How do you know? What evidence of learning do you see in their work or the notes you collected from the discussion?

What would you change or improve about your lesson?

Share a positive moment from your teaching experience.

What did you learn from this experience?

Let's get talking

With a partner, discuss the question:

How did teaching younger students add to or improve your understanding of interdependence?

After the project

You have completed your project!

Write and share your ideas to help you remember what we have learned and why it is important.

What are you most proud of in this project?

____

____

What skills did you practise during this project?

____

____

Why is treating nature with respect and as a source of ideas important for our future?

____

____

Create a drawing that reminds others about our interdependence.

Think about what you need to do to achieve your goals.

Do one good thing for Earth every day!

Rescue mission

Which sub-system are you designing? Tick (✓) the sub-system.

☐ **Water systems:** use and recycling of water

☐ **Crew quarters:** sleeping space, living and social spaces, happiness and needs of crew members

☐ **Greenhouse:** plants for oxygen and food, medicine, and other purposes

☐ **Animal quarters:** live animals, fish, worms, and so on

☐ **Solid waste systems:** human and animal waste, other recycling, and rubbish bins

Think about the inputs and outputs for your sub-system. To survive a long time in space, you need to make sure that every output becomes an input, and every input comes from an output. Your resources are only what you have on your spaceship. When you are in space, you cannot get new resources!

List them in the chart on page 86.

Use the design questions below for that sub-system to help your thinking. Discuss and plan connections to other sub-systems.

Water systems: What will you use water for on the spaceship? Where could the water come from? How do you keep the water clean so that you can reuse it?

____

____

Crew quarters: What do you think people will need and want so that they can thrive during their time on the spaceship? What about exercise, social, and free-time activities?

____

____

Greenhouse: What plants will you grow and why? Can you eat all the plants? Could they be useful for any other purpose? How do these plants grow and what do they require?

Animal quarters: What animals will you have? Why will you have them? What does each animal need?

Solid waste systems: Where will the waste come from? Is there a difference in the treatment of human, animal, and non-organic waste? How can you reduce, reuse, or recycle waste?

Overall: How will the sub-systems connect? How will you organize the spaceship so that inputs and outputs cycle?

Make sure all the sub-systems are functioning together!

Sub-system:		
Inputs	**Outputs**	**Ideas to recycle, reuse, and connect with other sub-systems**
E.g. Drinking water	*Urine*	*You can filter and reuse urine in the greenhouse for the fish farm tank.*

Draw and label your sub-system:

Laws and principles from nature

Natural processes are events and interactions that happen in nature, among animals, plants, and the environment. They make life happen. Natural processes happen on their own (people do not cause them), but they have important effects on humans.

Examples of natural processes include:

- photosynthesis
- decomposition
- pollination
- weather
- natural disturbances like earthquakes, storms, and floods
- the water cycle
- soil formation
- weathering and the rock cycle
- changes in the seasons
- life cycles.

Directions: For each picture, describe what you notice and what natural processes are happening. Look back at the bigger pictures on page 14 and 15 if you need to.

Use the list below to match the principle to the natural process you can see. Each picture may represent more than one law or principle from nature.

Some laws and principles from nature

- Nature uses sunlight and sugar.
- Nature recycles everything because there is no such place as 'away'.
- Nature thrives on diversity.
- Nature uses the power of limits.
- In nature, everything and everyone is interdependent and interconnected.

Activity page for Lesson 4 (page 14)

Picture 1

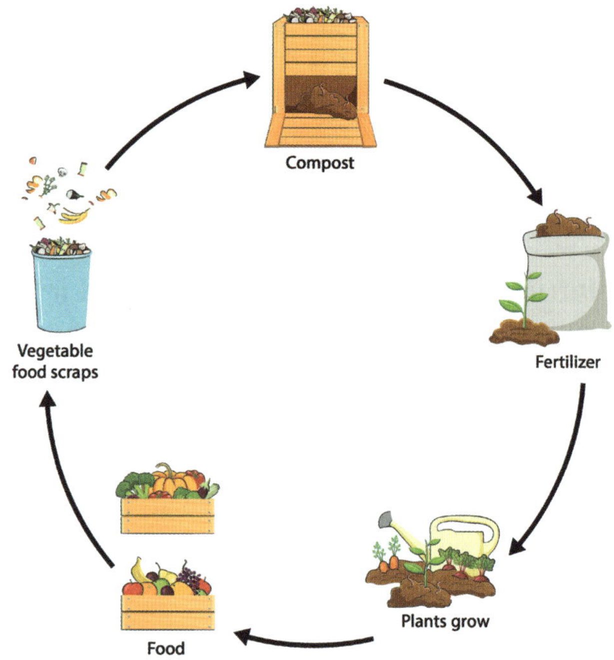

What do you notice? What natural process is happening?

What is the principle that describes this process?

Picture 2

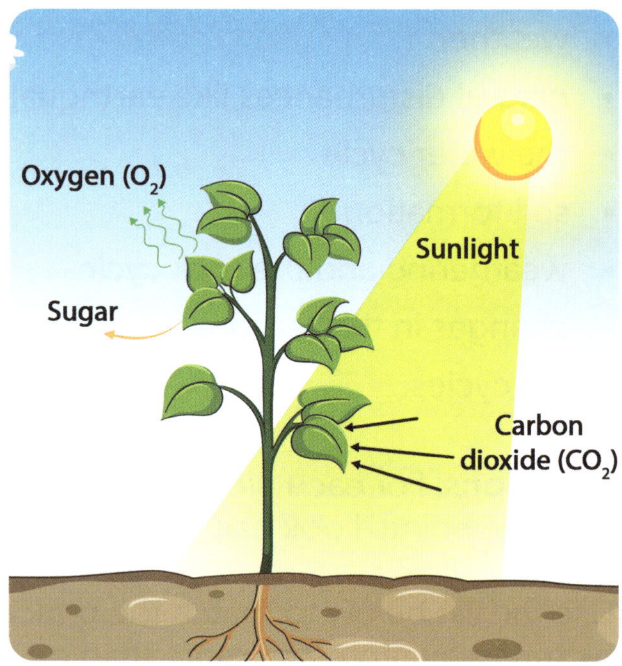

What do you notice? What natural process is happening?

What is the principle that describes this process?

Picture 3

What do you notice? What natural process is happening?

What is the principle that describes this process?

Picture 4 (Challenge)

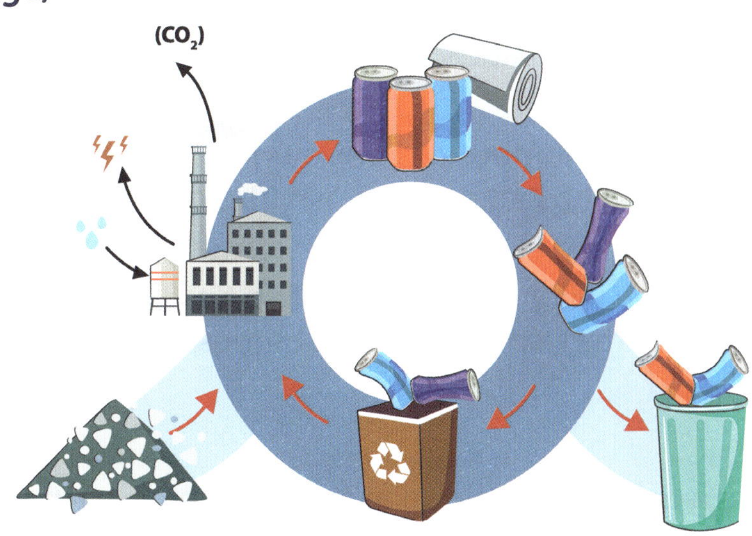

What do you notice? What process is happening?

What is the principle that drives this process?

Fishing Game rules

We are going to run a swordfish fishing industry!

Your tables are now oceans. Each person in the group will fish for swordfish in the same ocean.

Each group must choose a banker ('nature'), who will keep the fish cards from your teacher. The bankers will also fish.

The banker puts 20 fish in the middle of the table.

Twenty swordfish can fit in this ocean. This is the ocean's carrying capacity.

In each round, each person can fish for a certain number of swordfish. Traditionally, people fish for swordfish in the three following ways:

1. Harpoon fishing: take **one** fish
2. Long-line fishing: take **two** fish
3. Free-for-all long-line fishing: take **three** fish

Each turn, each person can take **up to** three fish, depending on the instructions for that game.

After each round, when all players have taken their fish, the banker ('nature') counts the number of swordfish left and adds 25% back into the ocean, up to but no more than 20 fish.

The added fish represent the number of baby swordfish made by the swordfish that were left after everyone has taken their fish (the ones that were left in the ocean to reproduce).

The aim of each game: You will play the game five times, each time a different way, and then again five more times, for a total of 10 times. The winner is the player with the most fish.

Game 1:

Everyone chooses a fishing technique at the beginning of the game and sticks with this technique until the end of the game.

Game 2:

Everyone chooses a fishing technique but can change technique each turn during the game.

Game 3:

The government has regulated for everyone. No one can take more than one fish each round.

Game 4:

A town meeting takes place so that you can discuss the situation and work together to come up with a good, creative plan that suits everyone.

Game 5:

As per Game 4 but at the end of each round, add 10% instead of 25%. (You still can't put back more than 20 fish, which is the ocean's limit or carrying capacity.)

Record-keeping sheet

Round	Consumption *(Number of fish you took this round)*	Accumulation *(Total number of fish you have)*	Fish stock *(Number of fish in the ocean after restocking)*	Other notes
1.				
2.				
3.				
4.				
5.				
6.				
7.				
8.				
9.				
10.				

Exceeding the supply

Part 1: Class work

Read: The carrying capacity of grazing cattle

Imagine that farmers in your area are allowing cattle to overgraze. Overgrazing is the practice of allowing animals such as cows to eat the plants on an area of land for too long so that the plants disappear completely. Once an area is overgrazed, the soil becomes very poor and it can take a long time for grass and plants to grow back. As a consequence, cattle cannot live in the area and the carrying capacity decreases.

In this example, how is the demand on the natural resources exceeding the supply?

Do the maths: what two things do we need to find out before we can find a solution?

What is one possible solution?

What type of agreement(s) would people need to make to achieve the solution? Who would have to agree to it?

Discuss: What happens if everyone changes their behaviour and keeps their new agreements?

Part 2: Individual work

Read: Water usage

Imagine a town where the river is running low because it hasn't rained for a long time. People have farms and gardens and need water for their plants and fields.

How is the demand on the natural resources exceeding the supply?

Do the maths: what two things do we need to find out before we can find a solution?

What is one possible solution?

What type of agreement(s) would people need to make to achieve the solution? Who would have to agree to it?

Scenario planning

Let's plan for the football scenario!

Discuss: What is the best-case scenario that has the most positive results for the most children? Write down your ideas.

Complete the table: What other futures are possible for the football scenario? Describe the best-case and worst-case scenario, and two other examples.

Best-case scenario:	Possible future X:
Possible future Y:	**Worst-case scenario:**

Discuss: Why do you think more children want to join the football team?

Talk with a partner: Imagine we are going in the direction of the worst-case scenario. What would we do? We must find a solution.

Practise flexible thinking and write down a few ideas for what you would do in this case.

Your preferred future: Scenario planning

Key question: ______________________

Certainties:

- ______________________
- ______________________
- ______________________

Uncertainties:

- ______________________
- ______________________
- ______________________

Law from nature: ______________________

Complete the table: What other futures are possible for the future of your community? Describe the best-case and worst-case scenario, and two other examples.

Best-case scenario:	Possible future X:
Possible future Y:	**Worst-case scenario:**

Comic: Our Future is Now

Create a comic about planning and working towards the best-case scenario.

Vision: Our preferred future ...	*One problem is ...*
What if we ...	*So that we ...*

Commons caretakers

1. Identify and explain three similarities between the ways people protected the commons in Apo Island, New Zealand, and Japan.

-
-
-

2. What creative solutions did people find in each case study?

-
-
-

3. How did people cooperate to protect the commons?

-
-
-

Connected commons

Choose one of the commons from the Local column and one of the commons from the Global column.

Local commons	Global commons
• Pollinators such as bees, butterflies, and other insects • Parks, public recreation facilities, or green community areas • Library • Plants and trees • Local wildlife • Public transport • Streets and pavements • Local languages and cultures • Community gardens and healthy soil	• Air • Water • Forests and wildlife • Languages and cultures • Knowledge

1. List specific actions that help keep the local commons healthy.
   - ______________________________
   - ______________________________
   - ______________________________
   - ______________________________
   - ______________________________

2. Explain how these actions could have a positive effect on the health of the global commons you chose.

____

____

____

____

____

Commons how-to guide

Read the list of actions in the first column below. Choose at least five of these actions. Write an example of a community doing this action to contribute to the health of their commons.

Think about the case studies and your own community.

Action	Explanation	Example
Make the community aware	Everyone understands and cares about the problem and what to do about it. Many people collaborate to find solutions.	**Example:** At Apo Island, community members and local leaders talked about the problems together.
Find inspiration and ideas	People ask for and accept new or different ideas from outside the community.	
Keep working over time	Community members keep working to improve and maintain the health of a commons.	
Check consequences	Be aware that when something is done to one part of the system, it affects other parts of the system.	
Let nature be nature	People provide the right conditions for nature to repair and revitalize itself.	

Activity page for Lesson 5 (page 43)

Action	Explanation	Example
Monitor results	Check if things are going according to plan.	
Recognize your errors and face challenges	People find ways to solve or get around problems and learn from mistakes.	
Keep an open mind	Different ways of thinking lead to better solutions.	
Learn from the past	Study the past to avoid making the same mistakes.	
Prepare for the future	Decide what changes are needed now to avoid problems in the future.	

Commons problems

Identify the specific problems in each commons. Think about solutions.

Scenario 1: The school garden

Describe the problems:

- ________________
- ________________
- ________________

Possible solutions:

Example: Create a weeding schedule for different groups of students to share the responsibility.

Scenario 2: The school library

Describe the problems:

- ________________
- ________________
- ________________

Possible solutions:

Activity page for Lesson 7 (page 46)

Scenario 3: The school playground

Describe the problems:

- ______
- ______
- ______

Possible solutions:

______

______

______

______

Scenario 4: The school pavements

Describe the problems:

- ______
- ______
- ______

Possible solutions:

______

______

______

______

Air quality guardians

1. Describe the air quality of your local area.

2. Would you say that your community's air is very polluted? Why or why not?

3. What would happen if *all* the air on the planet was polluted?

4. In what ways could polluted air from other places affect us?

5. Is air a limited or unlimited commons? Explain your thinking.

6. What can we do to reduce air pollution? Draw or write your ideas in the circles below.

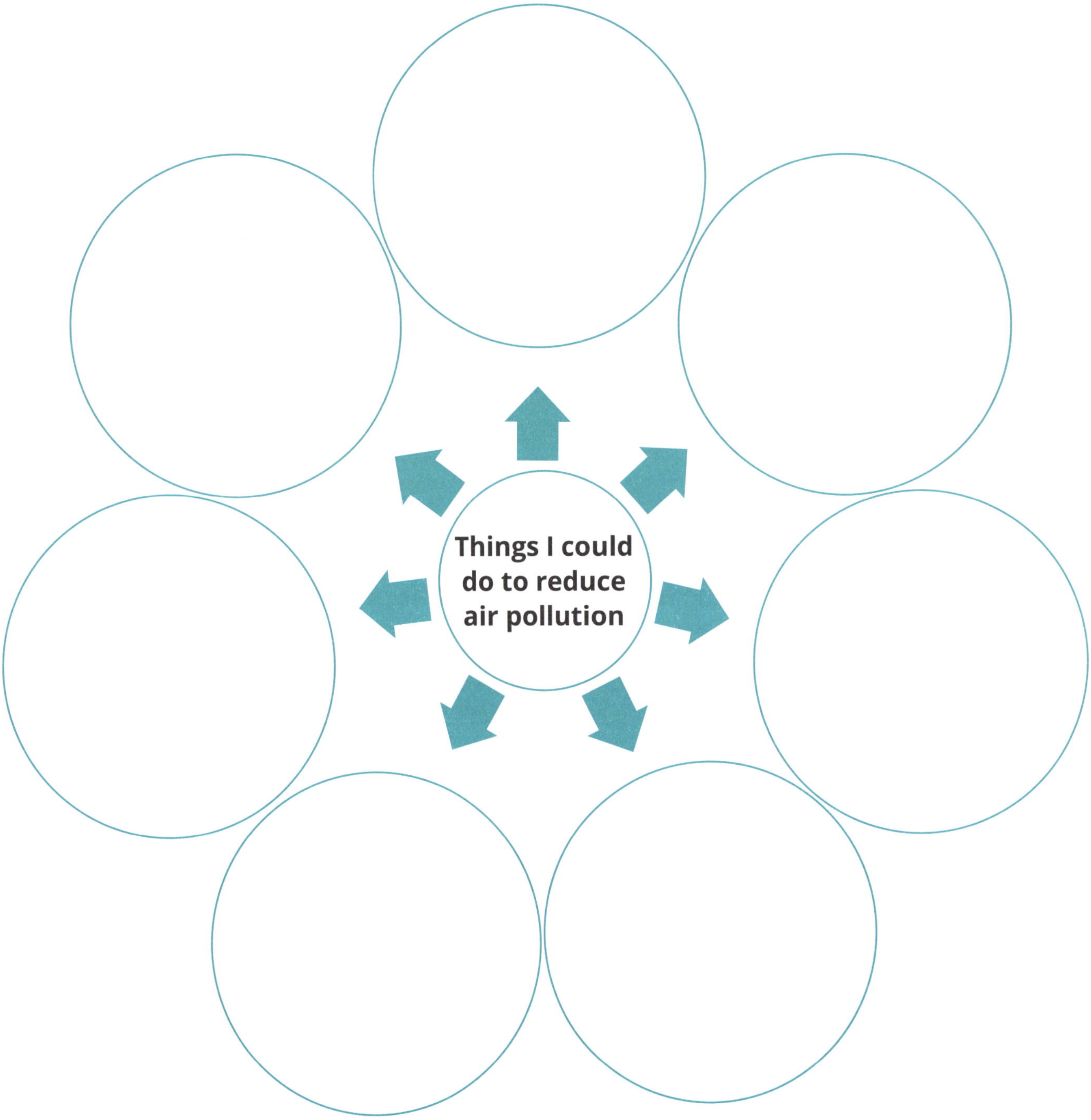

Our manifesto

Give your manifesto a title that reflects its purpose and that people will remember easily.

Title: ______________________________

Objectives:

Write 3–5 ideas for the manifesto.

- ______________________________
- ______________________________
- ______________________________
- ______________________________
- ______________________________

Design:

Consider how your manifesto will look. Use colours, pictures, or photos that relate to your commons.

On a separate piece of paper, draw and describe some design ideas to share with others.

How will you share your manifesto?

____

____

____

____

____

Design plan

Goal:

Describe the goal or purpose of your design.

Research notes:

Make notes on nature-inspired uses, strategies, and designs.

Possible solutions:

List different ideas and solutions based on what you learned from nature.

Plan:

Choose a sustainable solution, and explain how it is inspired by nature or uses the principles of biomimicry.

Design sketches:

Materials needed and steps for a prototype:

Write detailed lists.

Testing plan:

Describe how you will test how effective your design is.

Word bank

ability: the fact that somebody/something is able to do something

absorb: to take something into the body

activist: a person who works to achieve political or social change, especially as a member of an organization

adaptable: able to change to deal with a new situation

advisory: having the official role of giving advice

algae: very simple plants that have no real leaves or roots, and that grow in or near water

anther: the part of a flower that produces pollen

asthma: a medical condition of the chest that makes breathing difficult and which is made worse by air pollution

basic: of the simplest kind or at the simplest level; necessary and important to all people

biomimicry: using ideas from nature to solve problems

brick: a block used for building walls, houses, and other buildings

brief: instructions a person receives with a description of what his or her job is and what his or her duties are

canopy: the branches and leaves of a tree that are like a roof over the ground

carrying capacity: the most balanced number of organisms of a particular species that can live indefinitely in a system

certainty: a thing that is certain to exist or to happen in the future; the opposite is uncertainty, which is a thing that may or may not exist or happen in the future

circular economy: a system in which materials are never wasted but are recycled or reused

circulatory system: the system that sends blood and lymph around the human body

citizen: a person who was born or lives in a place

civil rights: the rights that everyone has to work, vote, and to be treated equally

consumption: the use of energy, food, or materials

cooperate: to work together to achieve something

coral reef: coral is a hard red or pink substance that grows on the bottom of sea and looks like stone plants; when there is a lot of coral, it is called a reef

crew: all the people working on a ship, plane, etc.

crew quarters: the part in a ship or spaceship where the crew lives

cycle: (noun) a series of events repeated many times, always in the same order

cycle: (verb) to keep changing and transforming during different stages

declare: to make a public statement

decline: (noun) a continuous loss of quantity, value, quality, etc. of something (opposite of revitalization)

decline: (verb) to become smaller, weaker, less good (opposite of to be revitalized)

deforestation: the process of cutting down large numbers of trees without planting new ones

demand: the quantity of something that people need or want to use or to buy

determination: the quality that makes you continue trying to do something even when this is difficult

diversity: many things that are very different from each other

dump: to throw something away and leave it in a place where you should not leave it, for example, by the side of the road

durable: something is durable if it lasts for a long time without breaking or becoming weaker

dynamite: a substance that explodes; it causes damage and kills living beings

ecology: the study of the relationships between all living things and their environment

efficient: working well with no waste

eliminate: to remove something completely

empower: to give somebody more control

estimate: to guess the amount of something without calculating it

exceed: to be greater than a particular quantity

extinct: a living thing is extinct if there aren't any individuals of this species anywhere in the world

facility: a building, service, or equipment provided for a specific purpose

filtration: a process we use to remove something we do not want from a liquid or a gas

flexible thinking: the ability to look at a situation and see it in a different way, or finding creative solutions to a problem

fossil fuel: a source of energy such as coal or oil that was formed over millions of years from parts of dead animals or plants; fossil fuels give energy only when we burn them, and they create large amounts of carbon dioxide and pollution

galaxy: a large system of stars and planets in outer space

gravity: the force that attracts objects in space towards each other, and that on Earth pulls them towards the centre of the planet, so that things fall to the ground when they are dropped

greenhouse: normally, a building with glass sides and a glass roof for growing plants; in your mission: in the part of the spaceship where you can grow plants

habitat: the place where a particular type of animal or plant is normally found

harmful: something harmful causes damage to somebody/something, especially to a person's health or to the environment

hazardous: something hazardous involves risk or danger, especially to somebody's health

importer: a person or company that brings products into a country from abroad

impose: to make somebody accept something they don't want to accept

inclusive: that includes everybody

indefinitely: with no ending point

indicator: a sign that helps us to measure change or the health of something

indigenous: the people who lived in an area before other people came there

input: that which is put in; any material put into a process or system

inspire: to give somebody the wish to do something

interconnected: with all the parts linked and working together

interdependent: when two or more people or things depend on each other

knot: to make a knot, you tie together pieces of string, rope, hair, or wool, turning them around themselves or each other and pulling tightly

law: the fact that something always happens in the same way in nature; a rule in society

lightweight: not heavy

limited: something is limited if its quantity cannot increase

lungs: the part of your body in your chest that fills with air when you breathe

mandatory: required by law

marine: connected to the sea

materials recovery: a process in which waste is sorted and separated into all the materials that can be recycled or reused

matter: physical substance of which everything in the world is made

nectar: a sweet liquid produced by flowers; bees use it to make honey

organics: materials produced by or from living things

output: what is produced

over time: with the passing of time

overgrazing: the practice of allowing animals such as cows to eat the plants on an area of land for too long so that the plants disappear completely

ozone layer: a layer of ozone, a form of the gas oxygen, high above Earth that helps protect Earth from harmful radiation from the sun

policy: a plan of action agreed by a government or leaders in an organization

pollen: the part of a flower that is carried to other flowers of the same kind to make more flowers and produce seeds

pollinator: an insect that carries pollen from flower to flower

principle: a rule, or scientific law, that explains how something works or why it happens; you use it as the point from which you develop other principles

prototype: the first design or model of something

radiate: to send energy out in all directions

reciprocity: when two people provide help to each other

recovery: the action of getting something back (especially after someone wasted, lost, or stole it)

reflect: to throw something back (for example, light or heat) from a surface

renew: to replace with something new

renewable: something that will never end because we can replace it or because we use it carefully; for example, wind power is renewable because we will always have wind; bamboo is a plant that grows very quickly, so if we cut it, we can replace it easily

replenishment rate: the amount of time it takes for resources to be restored and renewed

resilient: able to go back to working well after something bad happened

responsibilities: duties towards other people and the community

restore: to return something to its original state or condition

revitalize: to make something stronger and healthier

revitalization: the process of making something stronger, healthier, or more active (opposite of decline)

right: something that the law says you have just because you are living; for example, in a democracy, everybody has the right to vote and to education

rigid thinking: when it is hard to see a situation differently; the person wants things done only their way

ripple effect: a ripple is a small wave; a ripple effect is a situation in which an event or action has an effect on something, which then has an effect on something else, like the waves that a stone creates when you throw it in a lake

sanctuary: an area where wild animals are protected

scenario: a possible future situation

scenario planning: to make guesses about the future and to plan for all possible situations

sector: a part of an area of activity, especially of a country's economy

seed: a part produced by a plant from which a new plant can grow to replace them

self-cleaning: something that cleans itself

sensory: connected with physical senses

solar: of the sun, or connected to the sun

source: where something starts or comes from; for example, the source of a river is where it starts

spaceship: an aircraft that is built for going into space

sponsor: to give money to help an event or programme

stigma: the part in the middle of a flower that makes seeds if pollen goes into it

sub-system: a system within a system

supply: the quantity of something that is available for use or to buy

sustain: to provide enough of what somebody or something needs in order to live or exist

sustainable: something we can have or do for a very long time

systems: two or more parts that interact with one another over time and form a whole

terrestrial: of Earth, or connected to Earth

thrive: to grow and get stronger

to scale: when you draw something to scale, you make sure your drawing is exactly the same as the thing you want to show, only smaller

tree cutting: a piece cut from a tree that is used to grow a new tree

trust: trust is a feeling; if you have trust in a person, you feel that the person is good and tells the truth

unlimited: something is unlimited if its quantity never ends

untangle: to separate the parts of a knot

ventilation: how much fresh air is allowed into a room

vision: the ability to think about or plan the future with great imagination and intelligence

vulnerable: if you are vulnerable to an illness, you can easily catch it

waste: something that you throw away because you do not want it; solid or liquid material that bodies produce as a result of eating and drinking

wellbeing: general health and happiness

wildlife: animals and birds that are wild and live in a natural environment

within: inside

woodsman: a person who works or lives in a forest, taking care of and sometimes cutting down trees